Presented To:

Aunt Mary Crew

From:

Kathy, Mark,
Mike, Ty, Katie, Natala & Elsa

Date:

Christmas 2002

God Will Make a Way

Stories of Hope

by

INTEGRITY
BOOKS™

ALBURY PUBLISHING
Tulsa, Oklahoma

God Will Make a Way: Stories of Hope
ISBN 1-57778-099-X
Copyright © 1999 by Integrity Incorporated
1000 Cody Road
Mobile, Alabama 36695

Published by ALBURY PUBLISHING
P. O. Box 470406
Tulsa, Oklahoma 74147

Manuscript compiled by J. Dargatz, Tulsa, Oklahoma

God Will Make a Way

Stories of Hope

Contents

Introduction
Trusting God to Make a Way

When we go through terrible situations in life — whether a diagnosis of a horrible disease, a tragic accident, the death of a loved one, a painful relationship, rejection, or persecution — it is VITAL that we get a renewed glimpse of the eternal God. He is more powerful than anything we face and His love is without condition and without end. God alone is the anchor who holds fast in the storms of life.

Most people want to believe that God is with them, and that He is working on their behalf. Indeed, most people do believe that God is well able to meet their every need, no matter how great. Our struggle lies in believing God cares about *us* — personally and individually — and that He cares about us *right now,* in the midst of our pain.

When tragedies strike and there are no quick answers to our questions, we feel stripped to the core of our faith. It is a struggle to continue to believe and trust God — our faith needs help.

Faith is made strong by only one thing — the Word of the Lord. Whether the Word is shared by a loving friend or relative, comes leaping off the pages of the Bible as we read, is preached from the pulpit, or is expressed to us in songs of praise and worship — the Word is what builds us up on the inside, brings revelation, and renews our spirit.

May this book, based upon God's Word and the encouraging lyrics of the songs from *God Will Make a Way,* strengthen your faith to walk with God each day. Make yourself a cup of tea, put on the music from *God Will Make a Way,* and let the Holy Spirit minister to you as you read these heartwarming stories of hope.

He Will Come and Save You

Say to those who are fearful-hearted

Do not be afraid

The Lord your God is strong

And with His mighty arms

When you call out His name

He will come and save

He will come and save you

He will come and save you

Say to the weary one

Your God will surely come

He will come and save you

He will come and save you

He will come and save you

Lift up your eyes to Him

You will arise again

He will come and save you

Say to those who are brokenhearted

Do not lose your faith

The Lord your God is strong

With His loving arms

When you call on His name

He will come and save

He is our refuge in the day of trouble

He is our shelter in the time of storm

He is our tower in the day of sorrow

Our fortress in the time of war 🎼

Bob Fitts and Gary Sadler
© 1995 Integrity's Hosanna! Music

GOD WILL MAKE A WAY...STORIES OF HOPE

More Than Hoped For

Maria Vasquez entered the bank timidly. It had been two years since she'd left her village to move to the big city of San Paulo, Brazil, where she had hoped to attend college. In that time, she had been unable to find a job that paid enough over her living expenses to even cover the entrance exam fees. Her goal of attending the university seemed impossible. Now there was a problem with her bank account.

The bank manager was very friendly, so Maria asked if she could leave her resume. She said, "Yes," and a week later she was having an interview. The general manager was a woman who seemed rushed for time. She asked Maria to go to the other room and write a short composition about anything she liked on the back of her application.

Maria was stumped, so she went to God and asked Him to "make a way where there seems to be no way." Then it hit her! Write about the song! Sometime earlier, Maria had heard the song, "God Will Make a Way," and it had become her prayer. She couldn't stop singing it. She sang it in English, Spanish, and Portuguese. *No,* she told herself, *I can't use the song!* But she couldn't think of anything else. So she wrote her composition, ending with the lyrics of her prayer.

Back in the interviewer's office, she tried not to fidget in her seat as the other woman read. It seemed an eternity before the woman looked up from Maria's composition. She had tears in her eyes! "This is everything I needed to hear," she said. The interviewer wiped her eyes and said, "Get all of your papers in order. You will start to work next Monday."

As a result of her new job, Maria Vasquez was able to borrow the money to take her entrance exams. She passed and started college the next term. "God made a way," Maria wrote us, "where I didn't see one and where I didn't imagine that it could exist."

Based on a testimonial letter from San Paulo, Brazil.

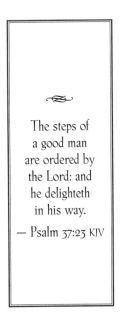

The steps of a good man are ordered by the Lord: and he delighteth in his way.

— Psalm 37:23 KJV

Meditating on God's Word through song brings powerful results.

Outside Help Required

Since thieves had stolen his navigational equipment, Walter Wyatt Jr. had decided to attempt the 65-minute flight from Nassau to Miami with only a compass and a handheld radio. In good weather, he could easily navigate his course with just these, but the darkening clouds ahead spelled disaster.

The storm rose more quickly than Wyatt had anticipated and when his compass began to gyrate, he knew he was headed in the wrong direction. He flew his plane below the clouds, hoping to spot something familiar, but immediately realized he was lost and in trouble. He sent out a mayday call, which was answered by a Coast Guard search plane. Directions were given to an emergency landing strip only six miles away from Wyatt's location.

Before he could make it more than a mile, however, Wyatt's right engine coughed and died. Wyatt could do nothing more than glide his plane into the water. It was 8:00 p.m. He survived the crash with only a nasty cut on his forehead, but his plane quickly disappeared below the surface of the water, leaving him bobbing in a leaky life vest. He spent the night kicking sharks away and fighting fear, and by morning he was nearing exhaustion.

Suddenly he heard the hum of an aircraft and the pilot spotted him, but it was twelve minutes before Wyatt grabbed the ladder of a Coast

Guard cutter. He climbed wearily onto the ship, where he fell to his knees in gratitude.[1]

Encouragement isn't what saved Walter Wyatt.

His intelligence didn't save him.

Physical prowess didn't save him.

All these contributed to his survival, but God saved him.

We cannot save ourselves. We cannot mend our own broken hearts. We cannot change our inner nature. Only God can do these things! Our part is to obey Him. We must look to the skies for rescue, and when that ladder appears, we must grab hold of it and start climbing!

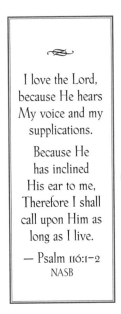

I love the Lord, because He hears My voice and my supplications.

Because He has inclined His ear to me, Therefore I shall call upon Him as long as I live.

— Psalm 116:1–2
NASB

The best place to send an S.O.S. is to heaven.

Giving Up the Questions that Have No Answers

"Why me?" That is the question asked most often when tragedy strikes or a problem becomes overwhelming. Tragedy strikes every type of person, good and bad, rich and poor, just and unjust. There is nothing fair about the fallen world in which we live. So the best question might be, "What does God desire to do in the midst of this situation?"

God's Word assures us that the Lord always desires to help us, deliver us from evil, save our souls, make us whole, and grow us up into the full stature of maturity in Christ Jesus. Every tragic circumstance, ordeal, or challenge has embedded within it the seeds that can produce something good in us and in those around us.

What if? What then? What about? These are questions of worry and anxiety. They are the questions we ask after the initial shock of a crisis passes and the suffering lingers. They are questions, however, that are beyond our human ability to answer. Only God knows the future. He alone knows all the possible results of any action we take.

There comes a point in any crisis where, if we are going to experience peace of heart and a rest for our souls, we must yield the matter fully to God and say, "I don't know, but You do. I can't, but You can.

I'm not able, but You are. And I know You will show me the way."

Elizabeth Cheney wrote a short poem that embodies our need to trust the Lord completely:

Said the Robin to the Sparrow:
"I should really like to know
Why these anxious human beings
Rush about and worry so."
Said the Sparrow to the Robin:
"Friend, I think that it must be
That they have no heavenly Father
Such as cares for you and me."[2]

We have a heavenly Father who cares for us with infinite care. He desires only that we trust Him so He may provide what we need.

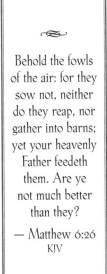

Behold the fowls of the air: for they sow not, neither do they reap, nor gather into barns; yet your heavenly Father feedeth them. Are ye not much better than they?

— Matthew 6:26
KJV

God has all the answers we need.

Living in Expectancy

Every night as he prepared for sleep, Dr. Horatius Bonar expectantly prayed these words: "Perhaps tonight, Lord!" In the morning, he awoke and prayed again: "Perhaps today, Lord!" For sixty years of full-time ministry, Dr. Horatius Bonar expected Jesus to return at any moment. While Jesus did not return during Bonar's lifetime, he did experience a *daily* coming of the Lord into his body, mind, and spirit; into the lives of his family members; and into the lives of those with whom he worked and worshipped.[3]

A similar story is told of a little boy who was very ill and whose parents were told by several physicians that their son had little chance of recovering. His grandmother, however, had told him Bible stories about how Jesus healed people, and each night the little boy prayed, "I know You are very busy, Lord, and have many things to do to keep this world from falling apart, but if You have a few seconds left over tomorrow, I'd sure like for You to come and heal me. I'll be looking for You."

For months the little boy lingered between life and death, and then one day, quite suddenly, he experienced a new surge of energy and vitality. The doctors were amazed as day by day he grew stronger and healthier. A full recovery was in sight after all! Several months after this dramatic turnaround, a physician asked the little boy if he had any idea what happened. "Sure," the boy said with confidence, "the Lord had a few extra seconds that day for me!"

For months, this little boy kept his eager expectancy that the Lord would heal him. He left the timing up to God, but he never lost hope that Jesus would come and deliver him from his situation.

Perhaps today.

Perhaps this very hour.

Perhaps right now the Lord is working in you the turn-around moment that you need to set you on your way toward a brighter and more joyous tomorrow. Be expectant!

But as for me, my prayer is to Thee, O Lord, at an acceptable time; O God, in the greatness of Thy loving-kindness, answer me with Thy saving truth.

— Psalm 69:13
NASB

Now is always a good time for the Lord to manifest His presence and power.

Christ Is With Us!

Anytime we are fearful or brokenhearted, feeling alone or weak, we do well to pray this prayer attributed to Saint Patrick. What a wonderful reminder that Jesus is *always* with us. It is up to us to open our eyes to see Him by our side!

May the wisdom of God instruct me, the eye of God watch over me, the ear of God hear me, the word of God give me sweet talk, the hand of God defend me, the way of God guide me.

Christ be with me.

Christ before me.

Christ in me.

Christ under me.

Christ over me.

Christ on my right hand.

Christ on my left hand.

Christ on this side.

Christ on that side.

Christ in the head of everyone to whom I speak.

Christ in the mouth of every person who speaks to me.

Christ in the eye of every person who looks upon me.

Christ in the ear of everyone who hears me today.

Amen.[4]

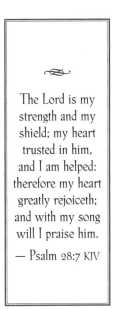

The Lord is my strength and my shield; my heart trusted in him, and I am helped: therefore my heart greatly rejoiceth; and with my song will I praise him.

— Psalm 28:7 KJV

Regardless of how you feel, Jesus is with you right now.

Sovereign Protection

The Lord protects us. Corrie ten Boom knew that truth well.

In her book, *The Hiding Place*, she tells of the tense period in Holland during the German invasion in the 1940's. On one particular night, Corrie tossed and turned in her bed while war planes roared overhead, shattering the blackness with artillery shells. Her sister, Betsie, also struggling with sleeplessness, decided the remedy was a cup of tea. When Corrie heard her sister in the kitchen, she arose and joined her. They drank tea and talked as shells exploded nearby. Finally the night became still again, and they decided to return to their beds.

Before lying down, Corrie reached out to pat her pillow. She felt something sharp cut her hand and discovered a jagged piece of metal about ten inches long. She cried out for her sister and immediately raced down the stairs with the shrapnel shard in her hand.

As Betsie bandaged Corrie's hand, she said repeatedly in awe, "On your pillow."

Corrie responded, "Betsie, if I hadn't heard you in the kitchen...."

Betsie interrupted, "Don't say it, Corrie! There are no 'ifs' in God's world. The center of His will is our safety."

Corrie later proclaimed this truth to millions in her book: "God's will is our hiding place."[5]

The Lord's arm is not too short to save us from evil — indeed, we are often saved from calamities when we don't even realize we are in danger. Thank the Lord today for His saving power. Praise Him for the many times He has rescued you, comforted you, and raised you up. Praise Him for sparing you from the snare of the enemy countless times in the past and future, even as you believe for Him to deliver you from the enemy's stronghold today.

Blessed are the people who know the joyful sound! They walk, O Lord, in the light of Your countenance.

In Your name they rejoice all day long, And in Your righteousness they are exalted.

For You are the glory of their strength.

— Psalm 89:15–17
NKJV

The Lord watches over you to protect you from all harm.

Brand Marks of Jesus

On August 8, 1981, Wendi Calton received what she calls "the brand marks of Jesus Christ." Returning from a high school church camp high in the California mountains, the van in which she was riding hit another car, went off the road, and dropped nearly two hundred feet. As the van landed the gas tank split, the van continued to roll, the engine set off sparks, and fire exploded everywhere.

Wendi was able to crawl out the rear window once the van stopped rolling. She recalls little of the fire, but more than half of her body was covered with third- and fourth-degree burns and her back was broken. The first person to reach her helped to keep her from going into

shock by singing with her, "Jesus Loves Me" over and over until the ambulance arrived. Later she learned that she was alone when the emergency medical crews found her. She feels certain she was helped by an angel.

Physicians told Wendi that she should have lost her right arm, right ear, and all the fingers of her left hand, but today she has all of these. Her back was healed, and so were her emotions. Over time, through surgeries, years of therapy, and a great deal of prayer, she began not to notice the burn scars that covered much of her body and face.

One day a friend shared Galatians 6:17 with her: "Let no one cause me trouble, for I bear on my body the marks of Jesus" (NIV). Wendi wrote, "My God is so big, I'm at a loss for words. He has brought me through the fire and He has delivered me from all the pain and baggage that could have followed me throughout my life."

Regardless of what you are going through today, the fact that you are *going through it* — are not defeated by it, destroyed by it, or killed by it — is a cause for great rejoicing. Not only is God saving you from all evil, but He is saving you from having a negative attitude toward what has happened to you. Praise Him for His total salvation!

Based upon a testimonial letter from Wendi Calton.

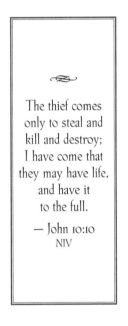

The thief comes only to steal and kill and destroy; I have come that they may have life, and have it to the full.

— John 10:10
NIV

Our marks of suffering can become badges of victory in Christ Jesus.

The Lion Sermon

Every year in October, a special service is held at St. Catherine Church in London. The highlight of the service is the sermon, which is preached every year. It has come to be known as "The Lion Sermon."

Sir John Gayer, who was at one time the Lord Mayor of London, had a reputation for being a godly man. Once while in Asia, he was traveling through a deserted area and his caravan stopped to rest. When the caravan moved forward without him, John ran to catch up to the others but suddenly came face to face with a large lion.

John knew immediately that anybody who could help him was too far forward to be of much good should the lion decide to attack.

God alone must be His deliverer! Instantly, he thought of Daniel in the den of lions, and he fell to his knees before the beast, shut his eyes, and cried to God to shut the lion's mouth. When he finished his prayer and opened his eyes, the lion was gone.

With great thanksgiving and rejoicing that God had delivered him from certain death, John returned to London and set aside a sum of money to be given away in gifts to the poor every October 15. With the donation, John asked that a sermon be preached every year on that date so that future generations might know that God hears prayer and delivers His people from evil. [6]

Although we may not be so keenly aware of the fact, we each encounter countless lions in our path during the course of our lives. The enemy of our souls has been likened to a prowling, roaring lion, seeking whom he may devour. There is no earthly power strong enough to defeat Satan, but thank God, in the mighty name of Jesus, we have authority over all the power of the enemy.

And then, what should be our response to the Lord's deliverance? The same as Sir John's response: an outpouring of thanksgiving and a freely shared witness that God hears the heart's cry of His people.

> Be sober, be vigilant; because your adversary the devil, as a roaring lion, walketh about, seeking whom he may devour: whom resist stedfast in the faith.
>
> — 1 Peter 5:8–9
> KJV

The Lord will shut the mouth of any lie'n lion!

Cast Thy Burden

Cast thy burden

Upon the Lord

And He shall sustain thee

He shall never suffer

The righteous

To be moved

As for me

I will call upon God

And the Lord

Will save me

Evening and morning

And at noon

Will I pray

And cry aloud

He shall hear

My voice 𝄞

Cheryl Seifert Natt
© 1973 Integrity's Hosanna! Music
Psalm 55:22,16-17 KJV

We Are Created for Worship

Cheryl Seifert Natt was thirteen years old when she was born again at a Bible camp in Minnesota. Those were the days of the "Jesus Movement" and for Cheryl and her friends, the Psalms became their songbook. Original songs and personally recorded cassette tapes were often passed along among those in her Bible study group and to others across the nation. Cheryl's own Bible became colorfully marked with the psalms she had learned to sing.

Cheryl taught herself to play the guitar, and in her personal quiet time she often took favorite Scriptures and put them to music. She recalls that she spent so much time doing this as a teenager that she began dreaming about writing songs in her sleep.

"Cast Thy Burden" was written while Cheryl was on a family trip to visit her aunt and uncle. She was sixteen years old, and after dinner with the family, while the grown-ups continued to visit downstairs, she went upstairs and put these portions of Psalm 55 to music.

Cheryl's song was a blessing to many people, but it became a blessing in her own life when she saw how it helped her mother again and again in her battle with lung cancer. This song in particular carried her mother through painful tests, an MRI episode (especially frightening because she was claustrophobic), pre-surgery fear, and chemotherapy. It continued to sustain her for years afterward.

Cheryl's mother was very pleased when the song was finally recorded, almost twenty years after it was written. God's Word had ministered to her so often through her daughter's song — she was glad to know that now it could be a blessing to many others.

Cheryl writes, "Music is so powerful because it was created by God for worship. It is not simply musical notes, but something spiritual. When music is combined with God's Word, there is nothing that compares to its power in worship."

As for me, I will call upon God; and the Lord shall save me. Evening, and morning, and at noon, will I pray, and cry aloud: and he shall hear my voice... Cast thy burden upon the Lord, and he shall sustain thee: he shall never suffer the righteous to be moved.

— Psalm 55:16-17,22 KJV

Something divine always happens when music and the Word are combined in worship.

Carried in God's Arms

A pastor was busy preparing his sermon in his study and his little boy was "reading" a book of pictures by the fireside in the room with him. The pastor realized that he needed a reference book that he had left upstairs, so he asked his son to get it for him. The little boy was eager to help and quickly ran out of the room.

After several minutes passed, the father noticed that his son seemed to be taking quite a long time to retrieve the book. He got up, walked out of his study, and stopped short at what he saw. His little son was sitting at the top of the staircase, crying. The book that the pastor wanted was lying at his feet.

"Oh, Daddy," the little boy sobbed, "I can't carry it. It's too heavy for me."

In a flash, the father ran up the stairs, stooped down, took both the book and his son in his strong arms, and carried them back to the study below.[1]

So often we attempt to do what God calls us to do in our own strength, not realizing that He never intended for us to do it alone. He desires for us to get where He desires for us to go by His strength, His wisdom, and His guidance.

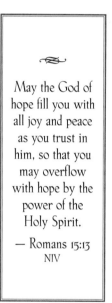

May the God of hope fill you with all joy and peace as you trust in him, so that you may overflow with hope by the power of the Holy Spirit.

— Romans 15:13
NIV

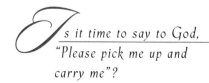

Is it time to say to God, "Please pick me up and carry me"?

No Matter the Need

Nancy Litchfield dreaded going to court, where she was suing her former employer. Although she knew she had been unfairly dismissed, her employer had accused her of not being Christlike by filing suit against him. Above all, Nancy wanted to be a good witness for the Lord, so she consulted two strong believers. Both of them confirmed that she was doing the right thing.

The night before the hearing, Nancy and her prayer partner prayed that Nancy's heart would be cleansed of all hatred and bitterness, and that she would not say or do anything displeasing to the Lord. Nancy prayed for her employer and his family. But while they were praying,

Nancy learned that her employer had submitted statements that were filled with lies and errors. She also received a call from her mother, telling her she was ill and unable to go with Nancy to court. Despite these setbacks, Nancy put her faith in God.

As she drove to the hearing the next morning, Nancy listened to praise music. God seemed to say, "It's okay. My grace abounds in the humble," and she began to weep. Suddenly, the sky seemed bluer, the grass looked greener, and she was at peace. In her words, she was "covered in a Holy Spirit calm."

The first miracle came when Nancy was allowed to present her case. She had filed five months after her termination rather than within the twenty-one days the law stipulated. Then, not only was she awarded an acceptable severance package, but she was granted permission to resume work in the industry from which she had been fired. (This had been in dispute since confidentiality was an issue in her field.) The outcome was far better than she had ever imagined it could be.

God stepped in and saved Nancy from the ruin of her career. Even more so, He saved her from bitterness of heart and paralyzing fear. The Lord is faithful over all things that impact His children. Trust Him today to come and save you from your overwhelming problems and fears!

Based upon a testimonial letter from Nancy Litchfield.

I heard and my heart pounded, my lips quivered at the sound...yet I will rejoice in the Lord, I will be joyful in God my Savior.

— Habakkuk 3:16,18 NIV

The Lord not only saves our eternal soul, but our entire life.

Your Divine Partner

D an Crawford, the successor of the famous explorer, David Livingstone, was known for carrying a copy of the New Testament in the pocket of his jacket. After he died, this poem was found penned on the flyleaf of his well-worn book:

I cannot do it alone!

The waves dash fast and high;

The fog comes chill around,

And the light goes out in the sky.

But know that we two shall win in the end —

Jesus and I.

Coward and wayward and weak,

I change with the changing sky;

Today so strong and brave,

Tomorrow too weak to fly.

But He never gives up, so we two shall win —

Jesus and I.[2]

The Lord asks very little of us other than that we allow Him to be our divine partner in every endeavor of life. He never asks us to shoulder a trial or difficult period on our own strength, intelligence, or effort. He always invites us to proclaim the great truth of the New Testament: "I in Christ and Christ in me."

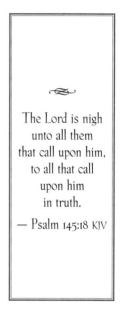

The Lord is nigh
unto all them
that call upon him,
to all that call
upon him
in truth.

— Psalm 145:18 KJV

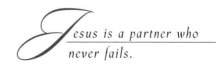

esus is a partner who never fails.

Setting Down the Heavy Load

A driver of a carabao wagon in the Philippines was on his way to market one day when he saw an old man carrying a very heavy load. The driver took pity on the man and invited him to ride in the wagon. The old man accepted gratefully and climbed aboard. A few minutes later, the driver turned around to see if the man was comfortable. To his surprise, he found the man still had the heavy load of goods strapped to his shoulders. He was still struggling under the heavy load, even though he could have been at rest.[3]

How often are we like that man? We say to the Lord, "I give my burden to You. I am trusting You completely with my life. I am not going to carry the weight of this load any longer." And then we continue to do all the things that we were doing previously! Here are some ways we cling to our burden:

- Talking incessantly about our problem without considering solutions.

- Blaming others for our own mistakes.

- Continuing to harbor bitterness toward those who have wronged us, refusing to forgive and continuing to speak ill of them.

- Seeking revenge and plotting ways to retaliate against those who have hurt us.

- Going to great lengths to avoid others.

- Crying out to God about our needs rather than praising Him for His provision.

- Calling attention to our problem or our need rather than praying for others.

- Seeking the assistance of others but never really allowing them to help us.

In these and so many other ways we continue to bear the burden of our pain, when God has invited us to ride in the cart of His love and provision. He wants us to let Him carry us and our burdens.

Don't continue to carry your burden! Decide today to set down your heavy load and enjoy what the Lord has for you!

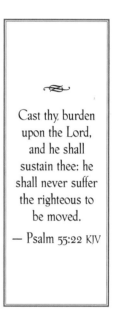

Cast thy burden upon the Lord, and he shall sustain thee: he shall never suffer the righteous to be moved.

— Psalm 55:22 KJV

Let go and let God.

A Burden Made Bearable

Jason White's life changed in an instant when he was diagnosed with an inoperable brain tumor. Then with the diagnosis of cancer came great restrictions on Jason's life. He was no longer allowed to work, drive a car, or mow the lawn. No medical hope was given him. From Jason's perspective, "It was definitely all up to God."

In the following months, Jason and his wife, Lori, learned many lessons from the Lord about His grace and faithfulness. The first was that God enlarges our capacity to endure suffering when we cast our burden on Him daily. He doesn't pour out peace and strength in weekly, monthly, or annual doses. Our walk with the Lord is always a daily walk.

God often sends others who can help us carry our burden. Jason underwent radiation treatments every day, Monday through Friday, for six weeks. Family and friends provided rides for him to the radiologist. Others provided meals for the family. Countless encouraging cards and phone calls were received. A trust fund was set up on Jason's behalf and, at the time Jason told us about his burden and the Lord's provision, the fund had four months' worth of salary in it. The Whites had also received an unexpected check for a thousand dollars. "Burden carriers" were gathering around Jason and Lori.

Above all, Jason learned that the Lord has an ability to carry us through difficult times and that nothing can separate us from our relationship with Jesus. Suffering and tragedies can become a great blessing to us if, through them, we come to be totally and utterly dependent upon the Lord for each day.

While he was still undergoing radiation therapy, Jason wrote: "I don't know if God will heal me. If He does, great! God works miracles. If He chooses not to heal me, that's great too! I get to go to my heavenly home. Either way, I win. I'd rather live a hundred days with God active in my life than to live a hundred years and never know He was there."

Based upon a testimonial letter.

God is our refuge and strength, an ever-present help in trouble. Therefore we will not fear, though the earth give way and the mountains fall into the heart of the sea.

— Psalm 46:1-2
NIV

The more we receive God's strength, the more we experience His grace.

Relying on God To Do His Part

Charles Spurgeon once preached what, in his opinion, was one of his poorest sermons. He stammered and stumbled through it and felt like a complete failure by the sermon's end. He was greatly humiliated, and when he got home he fell on his knees and cried, "Lord God. Thou canst do something with nothing. Bless that poor sermon."

All through the week, Spurgeon uttered that prayer about his failure. He awoke in the night and prayed about it. Then he determined that the next Sunday he would redeem himself by preaching a great sermon. Sure enough, the next Sunday the sermon was delivered well and, at the close of the service, people crowded about him and covered him with praise for it. Spurgeon went home pleased with himself, but he later said to himself, "I'll watch the results of those two sermons." And he did.

From the one sermon that seemed a failure, he was able to trace forty-one conversions to Jesus Christ. From the magnificent sermon, he was unable to discover a single soul who had been saved. [4]

In every difficult period of our lives, the Lord expects us to do the best we are able to do — to prepare ourselves as well as we can, to give our best effort to every task, to make the wisest decisions we can make — but He also expects us to trust Him to do what only He can do.

In the end, we cannot do God's work. We cannot save a soul. We cannot heal a body, deliver someone from evil, mend a broken heart, or make a person whole. We can do our part — give wise counsel, pray, lend a helping hand, be a shoulder to lean on — but we cannot do God's part. We must rely upon Him.

Casting our burdens upon the Lord means, in part, that when we reach the end of our abilities, we rely completely upon the Lord's abilities — not only to make up the difference, but to bring us to victory.

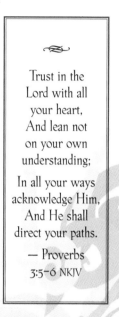

Trust in the Lord with all your heart, And lean not on your own understanding;

In all your ways acknowledge Him, And He shall direct your paths.

— Proverbs 3:5–6 NKJV

Producing anything of lasting or genuine value requires God's touch.

The Blessing in the Storm

Years ago a fishing fleet went out from a small harbor in Newfoundland, and by late afternoon the fleet suddenly found itself in the midst of a terrible storm. That night, not a single vessel of the fleet had found its way back into port. All night, the wives, mothers, children, and sweethearts of those who were on the boats walked up and down the beach, wringing their hands and calling on God to save their loved ones. To add to the horror of the situation, one of the cottages in the village caught fire. Since nearly all the men were away at sea, there wasn't enough manpower to fight the fire and save the house.

When morning came, to the joy of everybody in the village, the entire fleet had found its way safely back to the bay. The woman whose home had been destroyed in the fire greeted her husband with mixed emotions. While she was happy to see him, she was also devastated at the loss of her home. "Oh, husband," she cried, "we are ruined! Our home and all it contained were destroyed by a fire last night."

The man answered, "Thank God for the fire! It was the light of our burning cottage that guided the whole fleet back into safety and away from the rocks that would have ripped our boats apart!"[5]

No matter what we experience, God has a way of turning our worst moments into blessings. Trust Him to bring good out of every difficult situation you find yourself in — including the one you are facing today. He has a way to turn it around for you!

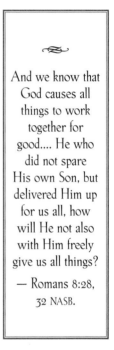

And we know that God causes all things to work together for good.... He who did not spare His own Son, but delivered Him up for us all, how will He not also with Him freely give us all things?

— Romans 8:28, 32 NASB.

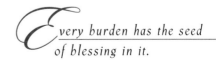

Every burden has the seed of blessing in it.

 ## Bearing the Burden of Another

There is an ancient legend about two brothers who owned and farmed wheat on the part of the mountain where the Temple of Jerusalem was built. One of the brothers was married and had a family, and the other brother was single.

On the night after one particular wheat harvest — the wheat having been gathered into separate piles of shocks — the married brother said to his wife, "My younger brother is lonely because he has no family and he is in need of a blessing. I am going to take a shock of my wheat and place it among his shocks as a special gift to him."

Meanwhile, the unmarried brother said to himself, "My brother is married and has the burden of caring for a family — I feel sure he could use an added blessing." He then went out to gather up a shock of his wheat with the intent of placing it among the shocks of his brother.

The next morning, to their mutual astonishment, they each discovered that their own number of shocks remained the same. So both men resolved to take a shock to add to their brother's harvest allotment that coming night. But again, in the morning they were surprised to see their number of shocks to be equal. This went on for several nights. Finally, they each decided to stand guard all night to see what was happening. In the middle of the night, they discovered each other.

One of the best things we can do when faced with a burden is to help another person whose burden is greater than our own. Every act of benevolence expands our capacity to love and be loved, to bless and be blessed. Generosity of heart puts us in a position to receive from God and keeps our hearts full of praise and thanksgiving.

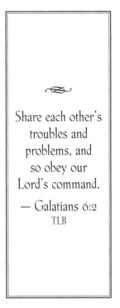

Share each other's troubles and problems, and so obey our Lord's command.

— Galatians 6:2
TLB

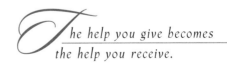

The help you give becomes the help you receive.

Be Strong and Take Courage

Be strong and take courage
Do not fear or be dismayed
For the Lord will go before you
And His life will show the way

Be strong and take courage
Do not fear or be dismayed
For the One who lives within you
Will be strong in you today

Why don't you give Him all of your fears

Why don't you let Him dry all of your tears

He knows He's been through pain before

And He knows all that you've been looking for

Nothing can take you out of His care

Nothing can face you that you can't command

I know that always you will be

In His love in His power

You will be free 𝄞

Basil Chiasson
© 1985 Integrity's Hosanna! Music

Courage to Hold On

On a commuter flight from Portland, Maine, to Boston, the pilot of the aircraft heard an unusual noise at the rear of the small plane. Henry Dempsey turned the controls over to his co-pilot and went back to check it out. As he reached the tail section, the plane hit an air pocket and Dempsey was tossed against the rear door. It became apparent all too quickly what the mysterious noise had been — the rear door had not been properly latched prior to takeoff. The door flew open the instant Dempsey hit it and he was sucked out of the small jet.

At that moment the co-pilot saw the red light go on that indicated an open door. He immediately radioed the nearest airport, requesting permission for an emergency landing. He reported that the pilot had fallen out of the plane and requested a helicopter to search the area of the ocean over which they had been flying.

After the plane landed, airport personnel found Henry Dempsey even before the emergency helicopters could take off. He was holding onto the outdoor ladder of the aircraft! Beyond anyone's comprehension, Dempsey had managed to catch hold of the ladder as he fell, and he had held on for ten minutes as the plane flew two hundred miles per hour at an altitude of 4,000 feet. As the plane landed, he narrowly kept his head from hitting the runway. Dempsey was holding onto the aircraft with such force that it took the airport rescue team several minutes to pry his fingers from the ladder.[1]

Whether it is a crisis situation or a time of sorrow that seems to have no end, there is no substitute for simply holding onto your faith in the Lord Jesus Christ. It takes strength to endure and courage to stand during the battles of life, but the Holy Spirit will give you both. And always, when the trial is over and God has shown Himself strong on your behalf, the victory is worth it.

I would have despaired unless I had believed that I would see the goodness of the Lord In the land of the living.

Wait for the Lord; Be strong, and let your heart take courage; Yes, wait for the Lord.

— Psalm 27:13-14
NASB

Knowing when to hang on and when to let go makes all the difference!

Prescription of Faith

Tan Khian Seng received two blows in a row: his mother had cancer of the throat and the doctor said she would need surgery. Nothing in the background of Tan's conservative Chinese family had prepared him or his loved ones for this. Tan's mother was filled with fear, not only of the cancer, but of the hospital and the surgery that her doctor had prescribed.

Where was God? Had He abandoned her? Could God be found in a hospital? She needed a healing miracle in her life, so would God choose to use surgeons to bring it about? With rampant cancer on one side and surgery on the other side, she felt completely blocked in. Where could she turn?

The day Tan's mother entered the hospital, Tan felt strongly impressed by the Lord to take a tape player with them. Throughout his mother's preparation for surgery and later, during the six weeks of recovery at the hospital, Tan played praise songs on the tape player. During every waking and sleeping hour, music filled his mother's hospital room with hope and encouragement. Her favorites were — "I Am the Lord that Healeth Thee" and "God Will Make a Way."

Hope is the gateway of faith, and as hope grew, faith grew. As faith grew, fear vanished. God used the music to part the waters of fear that swirled about the surgery, creating a path of faith on which Tan, his mother, and every member of his family might walk into freedom.

The surgeons were able to remove all traces of cancer, but it was the Great Physician — the Lord Himself, mighty and awesome in power — who truly healed Tan's mother and made her whole, strong, and well from the inside out, alive with faith and convinced as never before that no matter how formidable the foe and how dire the circumstances, God *will* make a way for those who lean on Him.

Based on a testimonial letter from Tan Kian Seng.

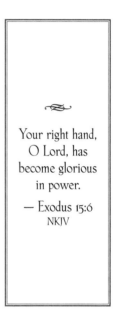

Your right hand, O Lord, has become glorious in power.

— Exodus 15:6
NKJV

When the Lord is present, fear must go.

Get Back Up

Several seasons ago during a Monday night football game, one of the announcers observed that Walter Payton, a great running back for the Chicago Bears, had just accumulated more than nine miles in career rushing yardage — a phenomenal feat. The other announcer underscored the accomplishment by noting: "And that's with someone knocking him down every 4.6 yards!" Walter Payton's average carry of the football was under five yards. His brilliance was not in long sprinting runs from goal line to goal line. Rather, it was in his ability to keep getting up each time he was tackled, and to keep running again and again and again.[2]

There is no shame in the number of failures we experience in our lives. There is no shame in the number of mistakes we rack up. Shame lies only in giving up and giving in. When we sin, we must never conclude, "I've sinned so many times I can never be forgiven again," or, "I've sinned to such a degree God will never want anything to do with me." God is always ready to forgive if you are willing to ask for His forgiveness!

If you've been hit and hit hard, you may need a little time to catch your breath. But then get up! Choose to move forward. If there are lessons you need to learn from the crisis you have experienced...learn them. If you need to grieve your loss or mourn the death of a loved one...do so, and in the process ask the Lord to heal your broken heart and to renew a right spirit in you so that you can live in vitality and joy once again.

If you need to make amends...make them.

If you need to get a fresh perspective or set new priorities...take advantage of this opportunity to get that new outlook and re-establish what's truly important to you and your loved ones.

Don't give up.

Don't give in.

Each time you get up from a hard hit, you'll find that you grow a little more resilient and a little stronger.

Be of good courage, and he shall strengthen your heart, all ye that hope in the Lord.

— Psalm 31:24 KJV

Being knocked down is painful, but choosing to remain knocked down can be deadly.

Word and a Prayer

Martin Luther King Jr. had this to say about courage and cowardice:

Courage is an inner resolution to go forward in spite of obstacles and frightening situations; cowardice is a submissive surrender to circumstances.

Courage breeds creative self-affirmation; cowardice produces destructive self-abnegation.

Courage faces fear and thereby masters it; cowardice represses fear and is thereby mastered by it.

Courageous men never lose the zest for living even though their life situation is zestless; cowardly men, overwhelmed by the uncertainties of life, lose the will to live.

We must constantly build dikes of courage to hold back the flood of fear.[3]

I do not ask to walk smooth paths
Nor bear an easy load.
I pray for strength and fortitude
To climb the rock-strewn road.

Give me such courage I can scale
The hardest peaks alone,
And transform every stumbling block
Into a stepping-stone.

— Gail Brook Burket[4]

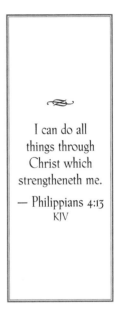

I can do all
things through
Christ which
strengtheneth me.

— Philippians 4:13
KJV

*Courage is not a feeling,
but a choice.*

The Father's Care

"I remember thinking several years ago, *Even though I don't come from a perfect family, at least we are together and we love one another.* Little did I know at the time that I was about to enter one of the deepest valleys I had ever known.

"Within the span of just a few short years, my oldest brother was killed in an automobile accident, my mother died from cancer, my youngest brother committed suicide, my grandmother died, and then my father died from heart failure. With each loss came a deeper and deeper sense of despair. I had many questions, fears, and regrets for lost opportunities. I wondered just how much more I would be able to take.

"Finally, I realized that even in my darkest hours, God had been with me all along. I came to the personal realization that no matter what tomorrow holds, I know who holds tomorrow! I know that no matter what difficulties may lie ahead, God will make a way!"

Solomon Smith has experienced tragedy and found His Father's care, and that translates into courage to go on living to the fullest.

If you are going through a difficult time, hold fast to the fact that your heavenly Father not only is walking with you, but He is the one who is holding you securely in His arms. Absolutely nothing can separate you from His loving care.

Based upon a testimonial letter from Solomon Smith.

> ❧
>
> For I am persuaded, that neither death, nor life, nor angels, nor principalities, nor powers, nor things present, nor things to come, nor height, nor depth, nor any other creature, shall be able to separate us from the love of God, which is in Christ Jesus our Lord.
>
> — Romans 8:38–39 KJV

The Lord always holds on to us tighter than we hold on to Him.

The Tide Will Turn

Harriet Beecher Stowe once noted: "When you get in a tight place and everything goes against you, till it seems you could not hold on a minute longer, never give up then, for that is just the place and time that the tide will turn."

The Bible gives us example after example of the tide turning "in just the nick of time." Even as Haman conspired to kill all the Jews in the kingdom of Persia and was building a gallows on which to execute her uncle, Queen Esther boldly took her life in her hands and begged the king to spare her people.

Even as the baby Moses was being set afloat in a basket in the reeds of the Nile River, God was compelling Pharaoh's daughter to go down to the river to bathe in precisely the place where she would hear the baby's cries.

When all that stood between the Israelites and the land God had promised to them was the Jordan River, God ordered Joshua to have twelve men carry the ark of the Lord into the waters. As they did, the waters of the Jordan dried immediately so that all of the Israelites passed over on dry ground.

As the wind-tossed boat filled with water and all aboard were in danger of drowning, Jesus calmed the sea with the command, "Peace, be still."

When Peter was imprisoned in Jerusalem and scheduled to be executed when the Passover feast ended, the Lord sent an angel to free him from the guards to which he was chained and guide him safely out of the prison.

The Lord honors our trust in Him to deliver us from all evil. We are commanded to trust Him without reservation or hesitation and to leave the outcome up to Him. We can rely upon Him to show us what to do, when to act, and how to respond even when it seems time is running out. Our trust in Him is a sign of resolve to be strong in Him and for Him at all times.

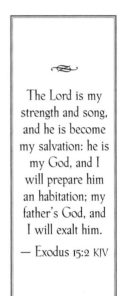

The Lord is my strength and song, and he is become my salvation: he is my God, and I will prepare him an habitation; my father's God, and I will exalt him.

— Exodus 15:2 KJV

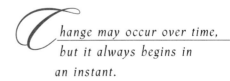

Change may occur over time, but it always begins in an instant.

Talk about Courage!

Felicitas was a noble, rich widow in Rome during the rule of Marcus Aurelius. She had seven sons, each of whom had accepted Jesus as his personal Savior. When Publius, the prefect of Rome, threatened Felicitas and her sons with death unless they worshipped false gods and denied Jesus, Felicitas replied that her sons knew how to choose between everlasting life and everlasting death.

One by one, the sons were brought before Publius, who demanded that they denounce their faith in Jesus Christ. Even as these demands were made, Felicitas encouraged her sons to stand firm and she reminded them of the everlasting and great reward that awaited them should they be killed.

One by one, they were executed. The eldest was scourged with studded leather thongs until he died. The next two were beaten to death with clubs. The fourth was flung from a cliff. The last three were decapitated. When the last of her sons had died, Felicitas praised God that He had given her seven sons whom He counted worthy to be among the saints in paradise and martyrs for His cause on the earth. Then, after prolonged and excruciating torture, she herself was beheaded.[5]

Did God make a way for Felicitas and her sons? Most likely, as each of these believers died, the Lord did for them precisely what He did for

Stephen, the first martyr: Jesus stood at the right hand of God to welcome them home. (See Acts 7:56.) There is no more glorious entrance to eternity.

God may not always make the way for us as we desire for it to be made. But He does always make a way for us that will bring glory to Himself and eternal reward to us.

> Behold, I send you out as sheep in the midst of wolves; therefore be shrewd as serpents, and innocent as doves...you will be hated by all on account of My name, but it is the one who has endured to the end who will be saved.
>
> — Matthew 10:16,22 NASB

God gives us supernatural strength to walk the path He has chosen for us.

Stay the Course

John Wesley was once asked what he would do if he knew he would die at midnight the following day. Wesley replied, "Why, madam, just as I intend to spend it now, I would preach this evening at Gloucester, and again at five tomorrow morning: after that I would ride to Tewkesbury, preach in the afternoon, and meet the societies in the evening. I would then go to Martin's house, who expects to entertain me, talk and pray with the family as usual, retire to my room at ten o'clock, commend myself to my heavenly Father, lie down to rest, and wake up in Glory."

That truth was echoed in a prize-winning poem in a contest conducted by the *Baltimore Sun* on the theme, "What would you do if you had one more year to live?"

If I had but one year to live;
One year to help; one year to give;
One year to love; one year to bless;
One year of better things to stress;
One year to sing; one year to smile;
To brighten earth a little while;
One year to sing my Maker's praise;
One year to fill with work my days;

One year to strive for a reward
When I should stand before my Lord.

I think that I would spend each day,
In just the very self-same way
That I do now. For from afar
The call may come across the bar
At any time, and I must be
Prepared to meet eternity.

So if I have a year to live,
Or just one day in which to give
A pleasant smile, a helping hand,
A mind that tries to understand
A fellow-creature when in need;
'Tis one with me — I take no heed.
But try to live each day He sends
To serve my gracious Master's ends.

— Mary Davis Reed[6]

Stand fast in
the Lord.

— Philippians
4:1 NKJV

*A consistent, godly life is
a courageous life.*

ourage to Believe

Courage says:

- If I don't experience a breakthrough today, I just may experience one tomorrow.

- If I don't find the answer I need today, I believe I will find it tomorrow.

- If I don't succeed on Sunday, I'll try again on Monday, and if I don't see results on Monday, I'll try again every day until I do.

- If the need isn't met by the end of this week, I will work and believe for it to be met by the end of next week.

- If nothing changes by February, I'll believe for a change in March, and if it doesn't come in March, I'll believe for it in April, and if it doesn't come then, I won't let up believing all year long and into the next year and beyond.

Courage is stick-to-it-iveness.

Courage is persistence.

Courage is refusing to give up.

Why are we to be so stubborn in our resolve? Because our courage is based upon the fact that God knows the answer. He can and will resolve our problem and meet our need. He will work all things for good in His timing, according to His methods, and for His purposes.

Courage is simply the stubborn face of faith.

> ∼
>
> Hold fast what you have, that no one may take your crown. He who overcomes, I will make him a pillar in the temple of My God, and he shall go out no more. I will write on him the name of My God and the name of the city of My God, the New Jerusalem,....And I will write on him My new name.
>
> — Revelation 3:11–12 NKJV

Tenacity is the essence of faith in God.

No Eye Has Seen

No eye has seen

No ear has heard

No mind has conceived

What the Lord

Has prepared

But by His Spirit

He has revealed

His plan to those

Who love Him

We've been held

By His everlasting love

Led with lovingkindness

By His hand

We have hope for the future

Yet to come

In time we'll understand

The mystery of His plan 𝄞

Paul Baloche and Ed Kerr
© 1992 Integrity's Hosanna! Music

Who Could Know?

As Joseph sat in that dark prison in Egypt, he couldn't help but feel betrayed. He had been cruelly betrayed by his brothers, falsely accused by Potiphar's wife, and forgotten by Pharaoh's butler. Who could know that the next morning Joseph would be brought before Pharaoh and be made the second most powerful man in all of Egypt?

That sunny day Moses was tending sheep in Midian, he couldn't help but feel forgotten. He had been a prince in Egypt. Then he had murdered an Egyptian and fled to Midian. Although he had enjoyed a good life with a wife whose father was a respected priest of the Midianites, he had been on the backside of the desert for forty years. Who could know that before that day was over, God would appear to him in a burning bush and within the year he would be leading two million Hebrews across the Red Sea to the land promised to them by God?

The night Hannah stood before the door of the tabernacle in distress, she couldn't help but feel rejected and empty. Although she enjoyed the love of her husband, she had not been able to conceive a child. Who could know that by the following year Hannah would bear a son who would become the greatest priest in Israel?

One day, four lepers stood outside the gate of their city under siege. They realized that if they didn't do something, they were going to starve to death. Who could know that as they marched toward the enemy camp, the Lord would amplify their footsteps and the entire army would run in terror? Who could know that by nightfall both they and those who were starving within the walls of their city would have all the food and supplies they needed?

God reveals what we need to know precisely when we need to know it — often in an astounding way. It may seem as if nothing is happening in your life. Don't be deceived! God is at work, and He has great plans for you...perhaps sooner than you think!

"For My thoughts are not your thoughts, Nor are your ways My ways," says the Lord.

"For as the heavens are higher than the earth, So are My ways higher than your ways, And My thoughts than your thoughts.

— Isaiah 55:8–9
NKJV

God releases His blessings to you as you are faithful to Him.

The Spirit Never Sleeps

One June morning, Sharon Staymer's life went on hold. Her husband was driving their two youngest children to their Christian school when a fully loaded dump truck came over the hill, lost control, and smashed into the driver's side of their car. Their son Michael was hysterical and had a large cut on his head, but was all right. Her husband had emergency surgery to repair a torn diaphragm, had multiple broken bones, none of which required setting, and he was covered with cuts and bruises. As painful as his injuries were, he knew he would recover.

The outlook for Jamie was less certain. She had a brain injury and remained in a semiconscious state. Her body thrashed about a great deal, and the physicians' best advice was to watch and wait. So Sharon began a personal bedside vigil in Jamie's room, continually playing praise tapes. Jamie had accepted Jesus into her life several years before, and Sharon believed Jesus would have no difficulty reaching her daughter's spirit even when she could not.

Sharon began to notice that Jamie was much quieter when the praise music was playing. Once, Jamie even tried to raise her hand to heaven as if worshipping God. This was a great sign of hope to Sharon as she wept, prayed, and waited. After six days, Jamie awoke. She went through a summer of intense therapy, and those who worked with her said they had never seen anyone improve more quickly from a head injury. That fall, she carried a full class load and was even able to resume cheerleading.

Praise touches a person at the deepest core of their being. The physical eye may not be able to see and the physical ear may not be able to hear, but the spirit never sleeps, no matter how badly a body may have been wounded or a mind bruised. Praise touches the spirit and renews hope and faith. And there is no limit to the healing power of the Holy Spirit working in the spirit of man.

Based upon a testimonial letter.

The spirit of man is the candle of the Lord.

— Proverbs 20:27
KJV

The Holy Spirit and the human spirit never slumber nor sleep.

 Keeping the Big Picture BIG

Often we get caught up in the day-to-day grind of life and lose sight of God at work — the big picture. We can become so concerned about experiencing an instant way out of our immediate difficulty that we miss what God is doing over time. He is certainly involved in the concerns of our individual lives moment by moment, but He is also accomplishing His own master plan for all of humanity. Each detail is part of a much greater, more elaborate, and grander scheme.

Nearly four hundred years ago, a shipload of travelers landed on the northeast coast of America. The first year they established a town. The next year they elected a government for the town. The third year, the government decided to build a road extending five miles westward into the wilderness. The fourth year, the people of the town decided to impeach their town government because they thought the road was a waste. *Why go there? Of what use is it? Who cares?*

Within five years, these people of great vision who had forsaken all comfort and family, traveled three thousand miles across an ocean, and overcame great hardships to explore a new land and create a new life had lost their vision for exploring what might be around the bend just five miles out of town.

God is not only involved in your life today — He has been involved in your life from the beginning. What is it that you once dreamed of doing? What is it that you once felt compelled to do for the Lord? What was once your deepest desire?

From time to time, we are wise to revisit the vision we once had for our lives and for the kingdom of God, the vision we had before we got bogged down in details, detoured onto side projects that were not part of our main purpose, or delayed by unexpected crises. We must keep the big picture of our lives BIG. We must see the whole of our destiny as God sees it.

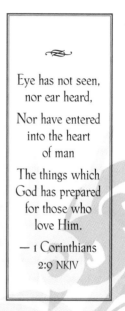

Eye has not seen, nor ear heard,

Nor have entered into the heart of man

The things which God has prepared for those who love Him.

— 1 Corinthians 2:9 NKJV

God never makes a plan that isn't grand.

Your Value

A person's value has been measured in many ways. The chemical, inorganic contents of a 150-pound man in the 1930's was estimated at 98 cents. Given inflation, the value of that same body has risen to about ten dollars. And yet we know it's worth much more than that. To the person occupying that physical body, it's invaluable!

In terms of education, the Institute of Life Insurance once estimated that a college graduate could earn twice as much in his lifetime as a high-school dropout, and thus, education increased the value of a human being. Yet we know a person's worth is not determined by the degrees behind his or her name.

It was once estimated that the atoms in the human body could produce 11,400,000 kilowatts of power per pound if they could only be harnessed. Yet we know a person's worth is not the energy represented in his or her cells.

The story is told of two families who shared a water pump. When the pump broke down, a quarrel arose between the families about who would pay the repair bill. One thing led to another and eventually bullets began to fly. Nine people died in each family. The total repair bill for the pump was 55 cents. That's only three cents per person. Surely we know that a person's life is not worth three cents![1]

What is a person worth? What is the unseen value of a person that cannot be weighed, measured, or priced? God says the value of a person is measured according to the shed blood of Jesus Christ. Nothing — absolutely nothing — is more precious or valuable to God than a person's eternal soul.

What has your mind failed to conceive about your own value before the Lord? Surely if you are so valuable before Him, He will take care of you, not only today, but tomorrow and every tomorrow thereafter.

[Jesus said], "Are not five sparrows sold for two farthings, and not one of them is forgotten before God? But even the very hairs of your head are all numbered. Fear not therefore: ye are of more value than many sparrows."

— Luke 12:6–7 KJV

Your value to God is beyond your ability to reason or calculate.

God's Clock

One evening in Albany, New York, a man asked a sailor what time it was. The serviceman pulled out a huge watch and replied, "It's 7:20." The man knew it was later, so he said, "Your watch has stopped, hasn't it?"

"No," he said, "I'm still on Mountain Standard Time. I'm from southern Utah. When I joined the navy, Pa gave me this watch. He said it'd help me remember home. When my watch says 5 A.M., I know Dad is rollin' out to milk the cows. And any night when it says 7:30, I know the whole family's around a well-spread table and Dad's thankin' God for what's on it and askin' Him to watch over me. I can almost smell the hot biscuits and bacon.

"It's thinkin' about those things that makes me want to fight when the goin' gets tough," he concluded. "I can find out what time it is where I am easy enough. What I want to know is, what time it is in Utah."[2]

One of the things we often overlook when we are hurting or struggling is that God operates on "eternity time." He is always looking at the whole of any situation and any person's life — all aspects, from start to finish, throughout eternity. When we find ourselves impatient, wondering why God has not yet acted on our behalf in the way we think He should have acted, perhaps we need to reset our thinking to eternity time.

When we find ourselves discouraged that we seem to be making no progress in our lives, and it seems as if we are just marking off the days on the calendar, we need to reset our thinking to eternity time. When it seems as if the night will never end or the storm will never pass, it's time to set our thinking to eternity time.

God is never too late or too early. He never operates too slowly or too fast. All things are done according to His perfect timetable.

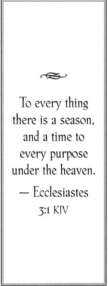

To every thing there is a season, and a time to every purpose under the heaven.

— Ecclesiastes 3:1 KJV

What time is it in heaven? The right time all the time!

$\mathcal{L}$earning to See What God Sees

A man from the eastern part of the United States was visiting West Texas one day. As his host, a rancher, drove him over the blistering and almost barren stretch of acreage that he owned, a large, brightly colored bird seemed to appear from nowhere and scurry across the road in front of them. The Easterner had never seen such a bird and asked immediately what kind it was.

"That's a bird of paradise," the rancher replied matter-of-factly.

The Easterner looked around. Seeing nothing but tumbleweeds and sky as far as the eye could see in any direction, he said wryly, "Pretty long way from home, isn't he?"[3]

We rarely see the full potential in anything God puts before us, be it a piece of property, a new job opportunity, an old house in need of repair, a relationship, a human being. We are nearsighted and shortsighted — we see only things as is. This is true not only in our view of other people, but of ourselves. We rarely have a glimpse of our full potential.

In sharp contrast, our heavenly Father has penetrating and all-encompassing vision. He sees all that can be, in the near future and in the long-range of everlasting life. He sees not only what we can become, but what He will help us to become.

Look for paradise in every place you walk today — see the potential for beauty that God sees. Look for what is good and noble and right about every person you meet today. See the potential for greatness God has placed within them. Look for what is worthy of praise and thanksgiving in everything you experience.

When you see the eternal potential in every experience, it will generate supernatural energy, hope, and faith. Your life will be infused with the wonder of God's love as He pours out His creativity through His people.

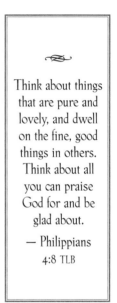

Think about things that are pure and lovely, and dwell on the fine, good things in others. Think about all you can praise God for and be glad about.

— Philippians
4:8 TLB

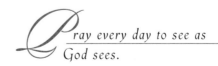

Pray every day to see as God sees.

Focusing on What Will Last

What happened to Alexander the Great's "Seven Wonders of the Ancient World"? A few pieces of the tomb of Mausolus, built in 350 B.C., can be found in the British Museum in London. The Temple of Artemis at Ephesus was destroyed in A.D. 262 by the Goths. The Hanging Gardens of Babylon have long since disappeared. The ruins of Babylon have been excavated in the twentieth century, but the splendor associated with the city is no more.

The magnificent statue of Zeus that once stood above the city of Olympus was dragged off and burned during the Byzantine era. King Ptolemy's famous lighthouse near Alexandria, Egypt, crumpled during a fourteenth-century earth-quake. The Colossus of Rhodes met the same fate in 224 B.C. when it toppled into the sea. Only the pyramids of Egypt have survived the ravages of time.

What man makes does not last forever. Last year's automobile styles are soon out-of-date, as are last year's fashions. Best-sellers and movie hits come and go year after year. Products break, things become obsolete, companies merge, tastes change.

When we look at the work we do, we could easily become discouraged, thinking that what we produce with our hands and minds will not last and is therefore of little benefit. That is far from the case when we are in God's will. While the things we produce, write, create, or manufacture are perishable, the work we do for the Lord always produces eternal results.

None of us are capable of seeing the full benefit of what we do. We cannot see the changes taking place in our own souls or the far-reaching impact our actions have on others. But we can resolve to live and work for God to the best of our ability, seeing our work as a continual opportunity to glorify Him in this earth.

The Bible tells us only two things on this earth will last for all eternity — God's Word and the eternal souls of people. These are the gold, silver, and precious jewels that will last forever.

Don't store up treasures here on earth where they can erode away or may be stolen. Store them in heaven where they will never lose their value and are safe from thieves. If your profits are in heaven your heart will be there too.

— Matthew 6:19-21 TLB

Every opportunity God sets before us has a treasure of eternity in it.

Optical Illusions

Is what you see what you get? Not always.

An entire room of a fifteenth-century Italian palace was once put on display at the Metropolitan Museum of Art in New York City. One wall of the room had twelve wooden cupboards whose open doors revealed about a hundred objects on the shelves, including an ancient hourglass, a celestial globe, old leather books, and various musical instruments. The wall space around the cupboards was paneled, and benches lined the sides of the room.

Unfortunately, some nearsighted visitors occasionally tried to sit on those benches, only to discover that the entire room was an optical illusion. Each wall was a flat surface.

More than 500,000 pieces of wood in various shapes and colors had been used to create the perspective and shadows that made the walls of the room look three-dimensional.

We may think today that we are looking reality squarely in the face, but unless we accommodate the spiritual dimension of any particular person, activity, event, experience, or relationship, we are experiencing an optical illusion. We are not fully seeing the plan God has in mind. The only way to see the world as God sees it is to ask the Holy Spirit to impart that ability to us. We cannot see as God sees by our own willpower or design. Genuine insight and wisdom come from within and are possible only as we allow the Holy Spirit to do His work in our lives.

What we regard as a failure may actually be the open door to a tremendous success. What we view as a limitation may truly be a protection. What we define as a trial may be a growing process. What we conclude to be a loss may actually be a gain. Only God can take the trials and tragedies in our lives and turn them into blessings.

Ask the Lord to give you His perspective and His understanding in every situation you face.

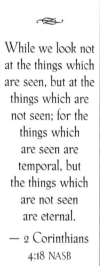

While we look not at the things which are seen, but at the things which are not seen; for the things which are seen are temporal, but the things which are not seen are eternal.

— 2 Corinthians 4:18 NASB

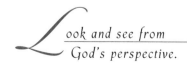

Look and see from God's perspective.

 *Jesus Knows!*

Joanne Rickels remembers the midnight phone call that told her that her oldest sister, Suzie, had been murdered. "The shock and horror that filled my heart that night stayed with me for many years. Family members and friends tried many times to help, but there was still a deep sense of pain within that I assumed I would always have.

"Finally, God got my attention and showed me that I had never *completely* surrendered to Him all my questions regarding Suzie's death. As I laid down all my questions of 'why?' at the foot of His cross, I saw a whole new meaning in Christ's suffering, His death, His resurrection. 'He bore our grief, He carried our sorrows, by

His wounds we are healed.' I came to realize that through Christ's tremendous suffering, God had already made the way for me to be completely free from the pain I held within! I was carrying a burden that He had already taken care of through the cross.

"As I laid my burden of questions and doubts at His feet, God fully restored to me the joy of Suzie's life and her laughter. There is no more pain in my heart regarding the events of her death!"

There is no pain that Jesus did not experience — physically, emotionally, mentally, or socially. He was rejected by His closest friends in His greatest hour of need, tried on false charges, tortured by both political and religious enemies, and then killed in an excruciatingly painful and publicly humiliating manner.

As Jesus sits at the right hand of the Father today, He *knows* how you feel. He's been where you are and He has endured what you are going through. So trust Him today to bring you through and let Him give you the comfort only He can give. As much as He knows how you hurt, He also knows how to heal you and restore your joy.

Based upon a testimonial letter from Joanne Rickels.

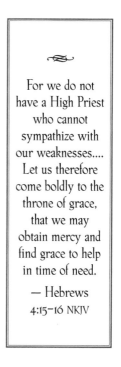

For we do not have a High Priest who cannot sympathize with our weaknesses.... Let us therefore come boldly to the throne of grace, that we may obtain mercy and find grace to help in time of need.

— Hebrews 4:15–16 NKJV

Complete surrender to Jesus brings freedom, wholeness, and healing.

You Are Eternal

You are eternal, unchanging
Your love forever will be unfailing
I can see You have a covenant with me
You are eternal, forever You will be my God

You are eternal, unchanging
Your thoughts and marvelous ways amazing to me
You will provide for every need
You are eternal, forever You will be my God

You will ever be the same

You are a God Who cannot change

And You have promised You'll never forsake us

You have called us by Your name

You are eternal, unchanging

And there is no shadow of turning with You

O it's true, I have a covenant with You

You are eternal, forever You will be my God ♪

Don Moen
© 1990 Integrity Hosanna! Music

God's Answer

He lost all of his children in a string of catastrophes. His wealth vanished overnight. He went from despair to despair, and his "comforters," his wife and three closest friends, did nothing but criticize and condemn him. Surely it was all his fault. Some secret sin he had committed. God was out to get him. And then his body broke out in sores that wouldn't heal and all he could do was scratch them, hoping for temporary relief. It had really been a tough couple of months.

We are all familiar with the story of Job's suffering. For 35 chapters we can read Job's prayers and complaints before God, his friend's reasonings and the theological debate over why he was suffering, and even his wife's advice to just "curse God, and die." Page after page the story goes on, confusion mounts, and things look as if they will never get better. Then God answers.

How did God answer Job? *With His presence.* He didn't explain why, He didn't apologize for what the devil had done, and He didn't wave His hand over the situation to put everything back the way it was before. He just came in His majesty and splendor and showed Himself strong. He let Job know, "I am eternal, I am your Covenant-Partner, and I am awesome. My love does not change. Is there anything I cannot do?"

Job was speechless.

In the midst of a trial, we struggle to understand. We create explanations for catastrophes, we rationalize events, we doubt God, and we blame ourselves. But God's answer is still the same as it was then, "I am here, and in My presence is fullness of joy."

Once God answered, Job prayed for his friends and showed them the path to God. His wealth was restored and doubled. His family grew again. He had seven more sons and his three new daughters became the most beautiful in the land. In God's presence was everything Job needed or desired — and God has not changed for us today.

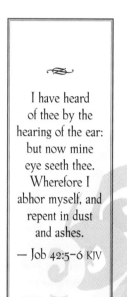

I have heard of thee by the hearing of the ear: but now mine eye seeth thee. Wherefore I abhor myself, and repent in dust and ashes.

— Job 42:5–6 KJV

Truly seeing the majesty of God answers every problem.

Comfort in Time of Need

Dave Berland was on his way to work at four o'clock in the morning on January 31, 1987. As he drove along the left-hand lane of the interstate, he started up a long upgrade — and that is the last thing he remembers about that morning.

According to witnesses, a van was parked on the median, half on the shoulder and half in the lane in which Dave was driving. He hit the right rear of the van, shot across the median and all four lanes of oncoming traffic, ran up the side of the hill to the right of the freeway, and then rolled back down into a ravine.

Dave was unconscious during most of the accident itself, but as he lay on the operating table, nervous and frightened, he asked the Lord to give him a word of comfort. The Lord spoke back to his heart in song, reminding him of the words of a praise tape he had recently received. The song spoke about the Lord being "a very present help in trouble." He closed his eyes and felt someone lay a hand on his chest. He didn't open his eyes, but instead held onto the hand. To him, that warm hand was God's own hand of protection on his life. A great peace engulfed him.

During his recovery from the surgery, song after song came to his mind. The Holy Spirit used music, which Dave had loved all his life, to comfort him and to build him up both spiritually and emotionally. The stronger his spirit and emotions, of course, the more quickly his body healed.

Physicians may be of tremendous help in a person's life. Wise counselors, those who pray with strong faith, and benefactors of all types are of help to us. But in the end, it is our Father God who is always there to provide the help that sustains, nourishes, and heals us to the innermost parts of our being.

Based upon a testimonial letter from Dave Berland.

I will not leave you comfortless: I will come to you.

— John 14:18 KJV

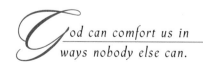

God can comfort us in ways nobody else can.

Cling to the Rock

A little boy and his big sister went out for a walk one day, and they decided to take a shortcut home by walking through a long, narrow railroad tunnel. For safety reasons, the railroad company had built small clefts next to the track in the tunnel so that if anyone got caught in the tunnel when a train was passing through, they might save themselves.

The little boy and girl had walked some distance into the tunnel when they heard a train coming. They were frightened at first, but the sister put her little brother in one cleft and she hurried and hid in another. As the train came thundering toward them, the sister cried out, "Johnny, cling close to the rock! Johnny, cling close to the rock!" After the train had passed through the tunnel, the sister went to retrieve her brother. They both were safe.[1]

No one in this life is immune from great trains of catastrophe and harm coming to destroy their lives. We have an enemy who is bent on making our lives miserable. Jesus told us that we had a choice: We could build our lives on the shifting sand of worldly thinking, or we could build our lives upon Him and His eternal promises. Either way, the storms would come, but if we built our lives upon Jesus, upon the eternal truths of His Word, we would stand.

We cannot keep the storms and waves of adversity from striking our lives, but when they come, we can cling to our Rock, Jesus Christ. We can be sheltered by the Rock of Ages, who is our strong arm and Savior, mighty and willing to deliver us from all evil.

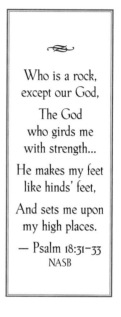

Who is a rock, except our God,

The God who girds me with strength...

He makes my feet like hinds' feet,

And sets me upon my high places.

— Psalm 18:31-33
NASB

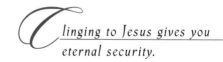

Clinging to Jesus gives you eternal security.

Glorifying God

Charles Wesley wrote one of the great hymns of the church on May 21, 1749, the eleventh anniversary of his conversion to Jesus Christ. The German Moravians had a great influence on Charles after his conversion. They were believers who loved to sing, were very missions-minded, and emphasized a personal conversion experience.

A Moravian leader, Peter Bohler, once said, "Had I a thousand tongues, I would praise Christ Jesus with all of them." Charles took that statement and built a hymn around it, not only to celebrate the date of his own conversion, but also to encourage others to give ongoing praise throughout their lives for their salvation and deliverance from sin's grip. He wrote:

O for a thousand tongues to sing my great Redeemer's praise,
The glories of my God and King, the triumphs of His grace!
Jesus! the name that calms our fears, that bids our sorrows cease,
'Tis music in the sinners' ears; 'tis life, and health, and peace.

He breaks the power of canceled sin, He sets the prisoner free;
His blood can make the foulest clean; His blood availed for me.
He speaks, and listening to His voice, new life the dead receive;
The mournful, broken hearts rejoice; the humble poor believe.

Hear Him, ye deaf; His praise, ye dumb,
your loosened tongues employ;
Ye blind, behold your Savior come; and leap
ye lame, for joy.
My gracious Master and my God, assist me
to proclaim,
To spread thro' all the earth abroad the
honors of Thy name.[2]

Every believer has countless reasons for glorifying God, but the foremost reason will always be our salvation. As we place our lives into God's hands, trusting Him to make a way for us where no way seems possible, we must always remind ourselves that there once was no way for us to be spared the deadly consequences of our sin.

All glory to God! He is the Savior!

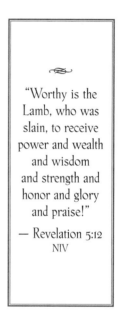

"Worthy is the Lamb, who was slain, to receive power and wealth and wisdom and strength and honor and glory and praise!"

— Revelation 5:12
NIV

Celebrate your salvation in praise and worship every day.

In the Presence of the King

George Frederick Handel's *Messiah* was first performed in London, England, on March 12, 1743. The king of England was present for the premier, and he was deeply moved by the time the performance reached its climax with the "Hallelujah Chorus." At the words, "For the Lord God omnipotent reigneth," the king could not contain himself any longer. Overwhelmed by the music and lyrics, he rose to his feet, and the entire audience joined him. They remained standing throughout the remainder of the chorus.

From that time on, it became the custom for audiences to stand whenever the chorus was performed. Queen Victoria, however, was advised shortly after she ascended to the throne, *not* to stand when she went to hear *Messiah.* Her advisers explained that the appropriate protocol was for her to remain seated, regardless of what other monarchs may have done in the past.

As the chorus began and the singers were proclaiming, "Hallelujah! Hallelujah! Hallelujah! for the Lord God omnipotent reigneth," Queen Victoria remained seated, with great difficulty. Then, as the chorus began to proclaim Him the "King of kings and Lord of lords" she rose suddenly and stood with bowed head, as if she desired to take her own crown from her head and cast it at His feet.

In the presence of the King of kings and Lord of lords we can do nothing less than stand in awe and praise at His majesty and bow before Him in worship. The glory of the Lord cannot be compared. It cannot be fathomed. It is higher, more awesome, more wonderful, more majestic than anything we can comprehend with our finite mind and limited senses. The glory of the Lord is from everlasting to everlasting.

Once we catch a glimpse of who is making a way for us out of our time of trial, all else will fade away. The more the Lord becomes the focus of our desire and our praise, the more our problems seem to dissipate.

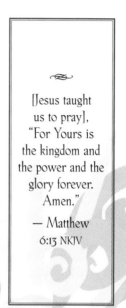

[Jesus taught us to pray], "For Yours is the kingdom and the power and the glory forever. Amen."

— Matthew 6:13 NKJV

The authority of Jesus Christ is absolute, including His rule over any problem you have.

A Personal River in a Desert

Jim Finefrock knows what it means to walk through a desert time in his life. For eleven years he was the technical director for a highly successful rubber company. He did his best to be a witness for Jesus, upholding truth and righteousness as he did his work. Then the company experienced an economic downturn, and just one month before the company collapsed completely, the Lord pulled him out. At age fifty, with a family to provide for, Jim found himself out of a job.

Even though his family and friends embraced him with their love and support, Jim found his ultimate joy in Jesus. In this desert of unemployment, the Lord led Jim on what he calls an "intimate, one-year journey." His journey was not a journey *toward employment* as much as it was a journey *with Jesus*. The Lord became his hiding place, his security, his provision, his comfort, his hope, his closest friend, his everything.

When the unemployment checks came to an end, God continued to provide for Jim and his family in sovereign and unexplainable ways. During the year, his son and two daughters enjoyed full celebrations of two graduations and a wedding. God made a way for them. Jim developed a new enterprise: The Christian Slide Service. Not all was joyful throughout the year, as Jim's father went home to be with the

Lord, but even in this sadness Jim knew, "God had made a way for him too!"

Today, Jim is working at a company close to his home and in the field where he had worked for many years. He says, "I still weep for joy on my way to work, because deep in my heart I know God has made a way for me."

During his time in the desert of unemployment, the Lord gave Jim Jeremiah 17:7-8 as *his* scripture to help him continue to believe and trust God to lead him to rivers in the desert.

Based on a testimonial letter from Jim Finefrock.

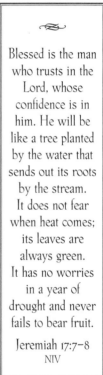

Blessed is the man who trusts in the Lord, whose confidence is in him. He will be like a tree planted by the water that sends out its roots by the stream. It does not fear when heat comes; its leaves are always green. It has no worries in a year of drought and never fails to bear fruit.

Jeremiah 17:7–8
NIV

God's answer to the desert is a river of joy.

When We Choose to Glorify God

While many of us know about Handel's *Messiah*, and perhaps can even join in singing parts of the "Hallelujah Chorus," few know about the life of the composer: George Frederick Handel. Handel was no stranger to suffering and tragedy. He lost his health and his right side became paralyzed. He became so financially destitute that his creditors seized him and threatened to have him imprisoned. He was so disheartened by the tragedies in his life that he almost despaired and gave up composing for a brief time.

It was in the shadow of being totally broken and devastated in spirit that this masterful musician undertook what was to be his greatest work, *Messiah*. Handel composed *Messiah* in twenty-three days. During that time, he immersed himself completely in the music, withdrawing from everything and everyone. In fact, even the food brought to him was often left untouched.

Handel was later asked to describe his feelings when the music and lyrics for "The Hallelujah Chorus" burst upon his mind. He said, "I did think I did see all heaven before me, and the great God Himself."

What a glorious thing happens when we put our focus on the Lord and upon Him *alone*. Everything else in our life recedes into the background, including our problems. The more we exalt and glorify God, the smaller our needs and problems become.

Faith rises easily in our hearts, and we know our heavenly Father will take care of us.

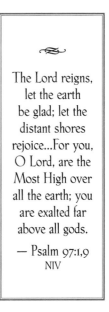

The Lord reigns,
let the earth
be glad; let the
distant shores
rejoice...For you,
O Lord, are the
Most High over
all the earth; you
are exalted far
above all gods.

— Psalm 97:1,9
NIV

Our faith is enlarged and empowered when we see God in all His glory.

On Our Knees

A young mountain climber was making his first climb in the Swiss Alps, accompanied by two stalwart and experienced guides. The young man was well-prepared for the climb physically, and although the ascent was steep and hazardous, he felt secure with one guide ahead of him and the other following.

For hours they climbed. Breathless and weary, they finally reached the rocks protruding through the snow at the summit. The guide leading the way stepped aside for the last few yards of the ascent so that the young mountain climber might have his first glimpse of the view — a wonderful panorama of snowcapped peaks and the bright, cloudless sky.

Clamoring up the rocks, the young man leaped to the top. The guide quickly grabbed hold of him and pulled him down. The young man had no way of knowing that fierce gales often blew across the summit rocks, winds strong enough to push him off balance. The guide quickly informed him of the dangers, saying, "On your knees, sir! You are never safe here except on your knees!"[3]

How true for us!

The safest and most secure place we can find on this earth is the place in the Lord when we are on our knees before Him. There is no room for pride, for there is nothing about the glory of God that we can earn or for which we can take credit. To glorify God is to exalt Him without any other thought in our mind or motive in our heart other than pleasing Him with our praise and worship. He becomes our everything, and the very atmosphere we breathe is God's presence.

It is on our knees that miracles are born and lives are transformed. We must never forget the awesome trust God has placed in us to pray, not just for ourselves, but for anyone He directs us to pray for. Truly, the place of power in the Christian life is the place of humility, on our knees.

Come, let us worship and bow down,

Let us kneel before the Lord our Maker.

For He is our God,

And we are the people of His pasture, and the sheep of His hand.

— Psalm 95:6–7
NASB

Do you want to experience the glory of God? Bow down and worship.

Revelations of God

Samuel F. B. Morse, the inventor of the telegraph, was once asked in a private interview, "Did you ever come to a point where you didn't know what to do next?"

Morse replied, "Oh, yes, more than once."

"And what did you do in those times?" the interviewer asked.

"I may answer you in confidence, sir," said Morse, "for it is a matter of which the public knows nothing. I prayed for more light."

"And the light generally came?" asked the interviewer.

"Yes, and may I tell you that when flattering honors came to me from America and Europe on account of the invention which bears my name, I never felt I deserved them. I had made a valuable application of electricity, not because I was superior to other men, but solely because God, who meant it for mankind, must reveal it to someone, and was pleased to reveal it to me."

Not surprisingly, especially when viewed in the context of Morse's faith, the first message that the inventor sent on his telegraph machine was this: "What hath God wrought!"

When God reveals His way out of our difficulty or sorrow, He will often give us great insights into Himself and into human nature (including our own nature). He will show us how He wants us to relate to Him and to our fellowman.

These insights are always for the improvement and advancement of those who receive them.

However, the insights God gives us about His divine majesty and provision are not to be retained for our own private benefit. The Lord intends for us to share these insights freely with all who seek to know more about His nature and character.

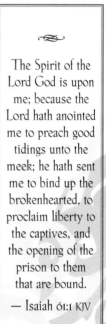

The Spirit of the Lord God is upon me; because the Lord hath anointed me to preach good tidings unto the meek; he hath sent me to bind up the brokenhearted, to proclaim liberty to the captives, and the opening of the prison to them that are bound.

— Isaiah 61:1 KJV

God delights as His glory is reflected from our soul back to Himself and onto others.

All His Benefits

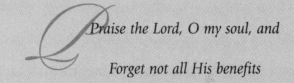Praise the Lord, O my soul, and

Forget not all His benefits

Praise the Lord, O my soul, and

Forget not all His benefits

Who forgives all your sins and

Heals all your diseases

Who redeems your life from the pit

And crowns you with love and compassion

Who satisfies your desires with good things

So that your youth is renewed like the eagle's 𝄞

Lyrics: Psalm 103:2-5 NIV
Music: Paul Baloche and Ed Kerr
© 1993 Integrity Hosanna! Music

"More to Follow"

The story is told of two men who worshipped God as part of the same church congregation. One of the men was poor, barely able to earn enough to support himself and his family, even though he desired to work and to serve God. The other man was rich, to a great degree because of an inheritance he had wisely invested and managed. The rich man determined that he would help the poor man, giving gifts to him through a friend so as to remain anonymous. With the first gift he gave, he wrote a little note: "This is yours. Use it wisely. There is more to follow."

A few weeks later, he sent a second gift with the same message. Over the weeks and months that followed, the rich man noticed that his riches didn't seem to be the least bit decreased. He also noticed that the poor man was still struggling; he still seemed plagued by problems in his health and misfortunes that were not always of his own doing. The rich man increased his giving, always with a note that said, "More to follow."[1]

What a wonderful picture of God's grace! There is always *more to follow.* We can never exhaust God's supply of care for us.

No matter how many times we are afraid, He comes to us and lifts us to safety with His mighty arms.

No matter how many times our hearts are broken, He reaches down to tenderly embrace us.

No matter how many times others attack us, He is always quick to become our refuge.

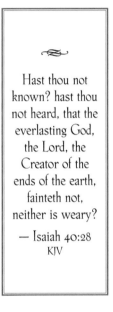

Hast thou not known? hast thou not heard, that the everlasting God, the Lord, the Creator of the ends of the earth, fainteth not, neither is weary?

— Isaiah 40:28
KJV

We can never exhaust God's supply of blessings for us.

It's Never Too Late

The "Old Colonel" had a reputation that was frightening, even to those who lived on the dark streets of New York City. At age sixty, he looked as if he were a hundred years old, and in many ways, he looked more like an animal than a human being. Clothed in rags, he wore an overcoat that was fastened with a nail. His hair was long and unkempt, his beard bushy and tangled. Although he once had been a college graduate and a brilliant law student in the office of E. M. Stanton, Lincoln's Secretary of War, the ravages of alcoholism and years of homelessness had taken a severe toll on both his body and mind.

One night he staggered into the Water Street Mission. To the amazement of those who had fed him periodically through the years, he cried, "O Lord, if it is not too late, forgive and save this poor old sinner!" God heard the cry of his heart and he was gloriously saved. Both his health and his intellect were miraculously restored by His loving heavenly Father, and the greatest love of his life, strong drink, became his greatest hatred. In the final years of his life, he became an honored and beloved Christian gentleman.[2]

What does this story illustrate to us? It's never too late to call on God! His benefits, through His covenant of love, are always before us. He can turn around the worst of situations in an instant. But we must first place our faith in Him and open our hearts to all He has already provided to us through the cross.

The mercy of the Lord is from everlasting to everlasting.

— Psalm 103:17
KJV

*Thank God that His mercies are new **every** morning.*

All That You Need

Maria Camacho and her childhood sweetheart were sixteen when they married. They both knew a great deal about the Lord at a young age, but once they married, they felt they were adults and could stop going to church and serving the Lord. Over time, the marriage began to fall apart. They began to use drugs, were broke financially, and generally felt miserable. By day they were able to hold down jobs, but by night they were controlled by cocaine, alcohol, and crack.

One night as Maria was getting high, her face, arm, and leg began to go numb. Scared and crying, she thought she would probably die before morning. In desperation, she cried out to God for help and forgiveness for her sins. She said, "Even if I am going to be paralyzed, I want to be back in relationship with You. Please forgive me and allow me to serve You."

God met Maria where she was. On Thursday, November 12, 1988, at 5:00 A.M., Maria was reborn. The heaviness in her heart began to lift and she felt more peace and love than she had felt in her life. She wanted to shout from the rooftop, "I belong to Jesus!" For the next two weeks, Maria was extremely ill as her body recovered. She wrote, "I am happy to say Jesus cleaned me completely, because when He does something He does it completely and perfectly."

A year later, Maria's husband accepted Jesus into his life and went through a program to overcome drug addiction. Maria's son, Johnny, also accepted Jesus. In Maria's terms, Johnny is "radically saved." Maria and her family consider their theme verse to be, "Finally, my brethren, be strong in the Lord and in the power of His might" (Ephesians 6:10 NKJV).

Maria believes strongly that while she and her husband may have wandered away from the Lord, the Lord never left them. He was always there waiting for them to accept Him as Savior and follow Him as Lord.

Based upon a testimonial letter from Maria Camacho.

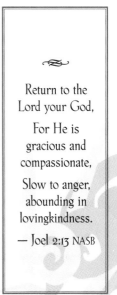

Return to the Lord your God,

For He is gracious and compassionate,

Slow to anger, abounding in lovingkindness.

— Joel 2:13 NASB

Only the Lord can satisfy the deepest hunger of the human heart.

The Origin of Praise

According to an old Jewish legend, after God created the world He called His angels to the throne room and asked them what they thought of His handiwork. One of the angels responded, "Only one thing is lacking — the sound of praise to the Creator." So God created music, and it was heard in the whisper of the wind, in the song of the birds, and in the babbling of brooks. Finally, the ability to sing was given to man. It is in praise and worship that the creation comes fully to life and is complete.[3]

We will never run out of things to praise God for if we keep our focus on His glory and remain in His presence. The more we praise God, the more we see clearly who He is, who we are before Him, and the relationship He desires to have with us. The more we praise God, the more meaning and fulfillment come to our lives.

Praise allows us to endure hardship until the moment of God's victory arrives.

Praise enables us to activate our faith to believe for God's definitive deliverance.

Praise makes us complete and whole and brings healing.

Praise gives us voice for our emotions when blessings, reconciliation, and harmony overtake sorrow, struggle, and strife.

Praise often is the way God designs for us to emerge from darkness and to stand boldly in the light of His love.

All Your works shall praise You, O Lord,

And Your saints shall bless You.

They shall speak of the glory of Your kingdom,

And talk of Your power.

— Psalm 145:10–11
NKJV

Our purpose in life is to praise God.

The Unseen Riches

One day the Reverend John Newton called upon a Christian family who had suffered the loss of all they possessed in a devastating fire. He greeted the wife and mother of the family by saying, "I give you joy."

She seemed surprised at his words, almost offended, and replied, "What! Joy that all my property is consumed?"

"Oh no," Newton answered, "but joy that you have so much property that fire cannot touch."

His words reminded her of the true riches of her life, those things that she valued beyond measure.[4]

From time to time, it is good to remind ourselves that the things we value the most are things that are unseen. They may be felt or experienced, but they cannot be handled, quantified, appraised, viewed, or calculated. The genuine riches of our lives include the love of family and friends, peace of heart, peace of mind, health, joy, hope for the future, and faith.

Where can you go to earn a dose of love?

Where can you go to buy faith, joy, or hope?

What can you do to acquire a shelfful of peace of mind or peace of heart?

We cannot count on things, possessions, or institutions to give us the true riches of life. To find them we must go to a Person. His name is Jesus Christ. He is the One who quickens in us all things that are of greatest value on this earth and in eternity.

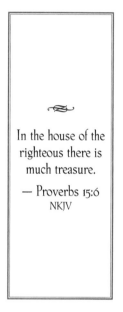

In the house of the righteous there is much treasure.

— Proverbs 15:6
NKJV

True riches of the Spirit can never be destroyed.

All Glory to God

When Gil Dodds, a minister's son, set the record for the fastest mile ever run on an indoor track in Madison Square Garden, he was asked to acknowledge the applause of the crowd by saying a few words. Dodds took the microphone and said, "I thank the Lord for guiding me through the race and seeing fit to let me win. I thank Him always for His guiding presence. I don't win those races. God wins them. You see, God has given me all I have. I have one great lack. I didn't have the one thing the coaches say a long-distance runner simply must have. I couldn't sprint at the end of the mile. But God took care of that. In place of the sprint, He gave me stamina."

Those who watched Dodds run agreed with him. He did not have a sprint at the end of his mile race; rather, he was sprinting the entire race!

God not only reveals His deliverance out of our troubles, but He also gives us the courage and the stamina to keep on until we experience a complete release from the chains that have bound us.

In areas where we are lacking in ability, He gives us the ability.

In areas where we do not know what to do, He imparts His wisdom.

In areas where we no longer have the stamina we need, He fills us with His energy and fortitude.

Our part is to acknowledge His help, without which we can accomplish nothing, and to thank and praise Him for the races He wins through us.

I will praise You, O Lord my God, with all my heart,

And I will glorify Your name forevermore.

For great is Your mercy toward me.

— Psalm 86:12–13
NKJV

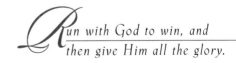

Run with God to win, and then give Him all the glory.

Sanctuary of Praise

Thelma Hyden's father, a dear man of God, was afflicted with Alzheimer's disease. As painful as it was for Thelma to watch him gradually lose his mental and physical abilities, she also had an opportunity to see that her father remained spiritually alive until the day of his death.

The very mention of the name of Jesus brought praise to his lips. He seemed to respond to Bible readings with understanding, even when other conversation and statements were confusing to him. The apostle Paul told the Colossians that the lives of believers are "hidden with Christ in God." (See Colossians 3:3.) These words took on new meaning to Thelma, especially in the last two weeks of her father's life.

Prior to that time, her father had been in full-time care in a ward with other Alzheimer patients. Then he suffered an intestinal hemorrhage and was confined to bed in a private room. Thelma took a compact-disc player to his room and every hour her father was awake, she played praise music for him. She had not been able to do this while her father was in the communal situation, as the TV or radio were always on and it was inappropriate to play music for any individual. But now, in his own private room, the family could minister to Thelma's father in *spirit*.

While the praise music played, Thelma's father lifted his arms in praise and worship to the best of his strength and ability. She could see on his face that he was enraptured at the presence of the Savior he loved and adored. The last two weeks of his life seemed to be especially anointed of the Lord so that Thelma's father might worship as he crossed over into heaven.

Praise is always our bridge from the confines and limitations of this earthly life to the boundless life we enjoy in Christ Jesus. Praise creates a sanctuary in which we can live fully in the freedom and joy of heaven, even while we are on this earth.

Based upon a testimonial letter from Thelma E. Hyden.

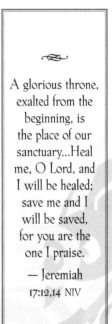

A glorious throne, exalted from the beginning, is the place of our sanctuary...Heal me, O Lord, and I will be healed; save me and I will be saved, for you are the one I praise.

— Jeremiah 17:12,14 NIV

Make praise and worship your sanctuary.

# Stepping into His Provision

One very rainy night, a woman locked her store and started home. There was a drenching, chilling rain and high wind. An umbrella was useless. The first trolley was late, so she waited on the corner for forty-five minutes. She was soaked to the skin and chilled to the bone by the time it arrived.

Two trolley cars later, she walked into her cold house. There were no dry clothes laid out for her, no warm supper awaiting her, no wood banked and ready to be ignited into a crackling fire. She thought to herself, *I usually have a happy disposition, but tonight I'm just going to feed my kitten and go to bed. I'm not even going to bother with supper. I'm just going to curl up and cry myself to sleep.*

As the woman removed her soaked clothing and put on her warm flannel nightgown and robe, the Lord brought these words of a song to her mind:

There is never a day so dreary,
There is never a night so long.
But the soul that is trusting Jesus
Will somewhere, somehow find
a song.

She began to hum the tune and then to sing the words aloud. In minutes, she had heated a quart of milk for her kitten and herself, had made a grilled sandwich and a bowl of soup, and had thrown a couple of logs into the fireplace and lit them. Without realizing it, she had created a cozy environment in which to enjoy her dinner and had spent a satisfying evening curled up with a heartwarming book.[5]

God does not make a way and then force us to walk in it. Rather, He makes Himself available to us as a source of courage, strength, and energy. We can choose to wallow in our misery, and in so doing, extend it and perhaps even enlarge it. Or we can choose to sing praises in the midst of our trying situation, and in so doing, extinguish the heaviness and move forward into joy and peace.

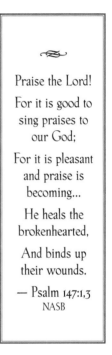

Praise the Lord!
For it is good to sing praises to our God;
For it is pleasant and praise is becoming...
He heals the brokenhearted,
And binds up their wounds.

— Psalm 147:1,3
NASB

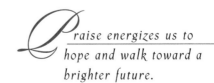

Praise energizes us to hope and walk toward a brighter future.

God's Best

Once when Caesar Augustus had given a very lavish gift to someone he desired to honor, the man was so overcome by the magnitude of the gift that he said to Caesar, "This is too great a gift for me to receive."

Caesar replied, "But it is not too great a gift for me to give."

Nothing is too good for you to receive as a believer in Christ Jesus. God does not desire for you to be whole except for one little weakness, one tiny flaw, one nagging and chronic ailment, or one small emotional hang-up. He desires that you experience His very best — every bit of His saving, healing, and delivering power!

God's power toward you is lavish, abundant, overflowing, and unspeakably wonderful.

He desires for you to experience all of His blessings to the fullest.

Don't discount your own worthiness to receive God's best. Jesus has paid the price for you to have access to the full storehouse of God's blessings.

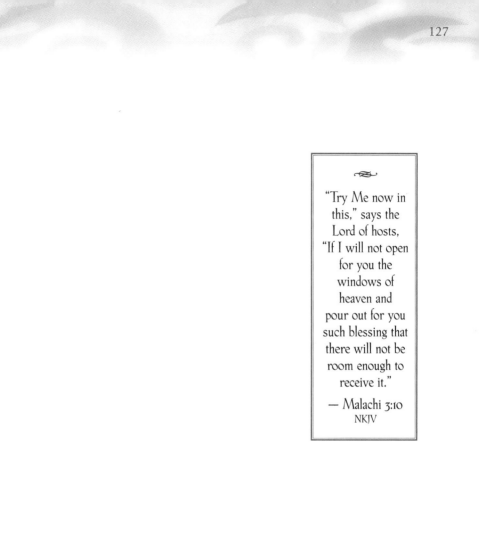

"Try Me now in this," says the Lord of hosts, "If I will not open for you the windows of heaven and pour out for you such blessing that there will not be room enough to receive it."

— Malachi 3:10
NKJV

Nothing is too good for a child of God.

If You Could See Me Now

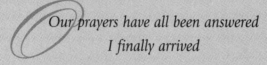Our prayers have all been answered
I finally arrived

The healing that had been delayed
Has now been realized

No one's in a hurry, there's no schedule to keep

We're all enjoying Jesus, just sitting at His feet

If you could see me now
I'm walking streets of gold

If you could see me now
I'm standing tall and whole

If you could see me now
You'd know I'd seen His face

If you could see me now
You'd know the pain's erased

You wouldn't want me to ever leave this place

If you could see me now

My light and temporary trials
Have worked out for my good

To know it brought Him glory
When I misunderstood

Though we've had our sorrows
They can never compare

What Jesus has in store for us
No language can share &

Kim Noblitt
© 1992 Integrity Praise!
  Music and Hold Onto Music

*O*ur Heavenly Hope

Although most of us do not like to think of death and heaven as being God's way out of our troubles, when we step back and view God's plan, heaven is His ultimate way to total and everlasting victory in all areas of life. The book of Revelation has a number of passages that speak of the life we will have in heaven. Meditating on these will bring an eternal joy to your heart.

And I saw a new heaven and a new earth: for the first heaven and the first earth were passed away; and there was no more sea. And I John saw the holy city, new Jerusalem, coming down from God out of heaven, prepared as a bride adorned for her husband.

And I heard a great voice out of heaven saying, Behold, the tabernacle of God is with men, and he will dwell with them, and they shall be his people, and God himself shall be with them, and be their God.

And God shall wipe away all tears from their eyes; and there shall be no more death, neither sorrow, nor crying, neither shall there be any more pain: for the former things are passed away...

And he shewed me a pure river of water of life, clear as crystal, proceeding out of the throne of God and of the Lamb.

In the midst of the street of it, and on either side of the river, was there the tree of life, which bare twelve manner of fruits, and yielded her fruit every month: and the leaves of the tree were for the healing of the nations...

And there shall be no night there; and they need no candle, neither light of the sun; for the Lord God giveth them light: and they shall reign for ever and ever.

— Revelation 21:1-4; 22:1-2,5 KJV

What a glorious future God has planned for those who are in Christ Jesus!

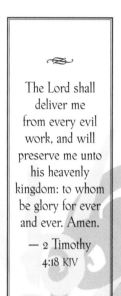

The Lord shall deliver me from every evil work, and will preserve me unto his heavenly kingdom: to whom be glory for ever and ever. Amen.

— 2 Timothy 4:18 KJV

Heaven is everything home should be.

132

Simply No Comparison

Alison Cooler knows what it means to be encouraged by the hope of heaven. She and her fiancé, Robbie, were involved in a head-on collision with another car. She survived with a few broken bones and minor internal injuries, but the next day she found out Robbie had been killed.

"I knew the Bible said God will not let you be tempted beyond what you can bear, so I believed that God would make a way for me to survive the emptiness and confusion I felt. The Lord works in many ways, often in a way we cannot see or understand fully at the time. As I prayed for God's help, various passages of Scripture came to my mind. Of special comfort to me were the Bible's promises of a heavenly home for those who love the Lord. I knew Robbie loved the Lord, and he was with the Lord. I also knew that when things seemed unbearable, I could trust God that He would make a way where there seemed to be no way."

The Bible assures us that believers in Christ Jesus are with the Lord after their death:

We are confident, yes, well pleased rather to be absent from the body and to be present with the Lord.

— 2 Corinthians 5:8 NKJV

I know the Lord is always with me. I will not be shaken, for he is right beside me. No wonder my heart is filled with joy, and my mouth shouts his praises! My body rests in safety. For you will not leave my soul among the dead or allow your godly one to rot in the grave. You will show me the way of life, granting me the joy of your presence and the pleasures of living with you forever.

— Psalm 16:8-11 NLT

Based on a testimonial letter from Alison Cooler.

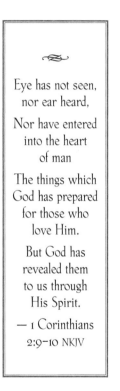

Eye has not seen, nor ear heard,

Nor have entered into the heart of man

The things which God has prepared for those who love Him.

But God has revealed them to us through His Spirit.

— 1 Corinthians 2:9–10 NKJV

No matter how wonderful life may be, eternal life will be infinitely better!

Heavenly Vision

Look where I would, I saw, half hidden by the trees, elegant and beautiful houses of strangely attractive architecture, that I felt must be the homes of the happy inhibitions of this enchanted place. I caught glimpses of sparkling fountains in many directions, and close to my retreat flowed a river, with placid breast and water clear as crystal. The walks that ran in many directions through the grounds appeared to me to be, and I afterward found were, of pearl, spotless and pure, bordered on either side by narrow streams of pellucid water, running over stones of gold. The one thought that fastened itself upon me as I looked, breathless and speechless, upon this scene, was "Purity, purity!" No shadow of dust; no taint of decay on fruit or flower; everything perfect, everything pure. The grass and flowers looked as though fresh-washed by summer showers, and not a single blade was any color but the brightest green. The air was soft and balmy, though invigorating; and instead of sunlight there was a golden and rose glory everywhere; something like the afterglow of a Southern sunset in midsummer.

— *Intra Muros: My Dream of Heaven*, by Rebecca Ruter Springer

Rebecca Springer experienced this vision of heaven during a period of great physical weakness and suffering. She made no claim to having gone to heaven or of having an out-of-body or near-death experience. Simply, she believed the Lord had given her a vision of heaven that produced great peace in her.

If mankind can envision such a glorious place this side of eternity, with the constraints of a finite mind and limited language, how much more glorious will our heavenly home actually be?

This is the greatest reward of holding on to the hope of heaven during this life: we experience *eternal peace*.

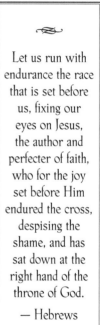

Let us run with endurance the race that is set before us, fixing our eyes on Jesus, the author and perfecter of faith, who for the joy set before Him endured the cross, despising the shame, and has sat down at the right hand of the throne of God.

— Hebrews 12:1–2 NASB

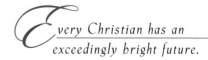

Every Christian has an exceedingly bright future.

Choice of Perspective

One day two women found themselves in a small, dirty village in rural Egypt. Travel plans had gone awry and they were forced to spend the night in a small motel room that had one bare bulb for light and a small, moldy bathroom that disgusted them. The one small window in the room had no glass, just iron bars. The conditions were the best the village had to offer, but a far cry from anything they had ever experienced.

The women chose to spend most of their two days in this village on the beach outside their motel room. There they found bright sunlight, the vibrantly blue Mediterranean lapping at their feet, graceful palm trees, and thousands of shells on the white sands of the beach. One remarked to the other, "Let's remember *this* as our experience in Egypt." They read the Scriptures, praised the Lord, and rejoiced in His protection and provision for them.

One of the women said years later, "I knew my stay in this village was temporary. I only had to close my eyes to envision the luxury of a bubble bath, clean clothes, and a soft, comfortable bed. I knew those things were only about a hundred miles and forty-eight hours away. I could endure that long! And in fact, I did not need to endure with an attitude of suffering. I could endure with an attitude of adventure. In many ways, I felt as if I were on a secret safari with the Lord."

No matter how bad a situation may be, there is always something of spiritual benefit if we abide in God's Word, our hearts are praising the Lord, and we are praying without ceasing. And a vision of better days ahead in heaven enables us to endure any present difficulty.

We always have a choice: Through what perspective will we view our circumstances — in light of our present discomfort or in light of eternity? If we use our sufferings to draw closer to God, we won't waste our life with selfish complaints, but we will turn adversity into everlasting joy.

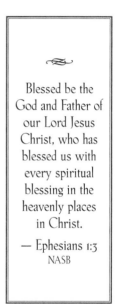

Blessed be the God and Father of our Lord Jesus Christ, who has blessed us with every spiritual blessing in the heavenly places in Christ.

— Ephesians 1:3
NASB

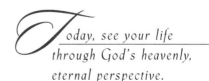

Today, see your life through God's heavenly, eternal perspective.

Take the Plunge!

We read in Revelation 22 about the great river of life, but that river is not limited to heaven. There is a river of eternal life that flows continually from Christ Jesus through us. When Jesus encountered the Samaritan woman by the well, He told her, "If you knew the gift of God and who it is that asks you for a drink, you would have asked him and he would have given you living water" (John 4:10 NIV).

The woman asked Jesus what He meant by living water, and He replied, "Everyone who drinks this water will be thirsty again, but whoever drinks the water I give him will never thirst. Indeed, the water I give him will become in him a spring of water welling up to eternal life" (vv. 13-14).

Later, while at the Feast of Tabernacles in Jerusalem, Jesus said, "If anyone is thirsty, let him come to me and drink. Whoever believes in me, as the Scripture has said, streams of living water will flow from within him" (John 7:37-38 NIV).

What did Jesus mean? The Scriptures answer that question: "By this he meant the Spirit, whom those who believed in him were later to receive. Up to that time the Spirit had not been given, since Jesus had not yet been glorified" (vv. 39).

An earthly river offers us two benefits: we can bathe in it, using the water to cleanse the skin, or we can drink from it, using the water to refresh and sustain the body. Both benefits of the stream are vital for our health and life.

The spiritual river that Jesus provides also offers two benefits: the Holy Spirit cleanses us from sin and comes to live within us in the new birth, and then He continually refreshes us with a flow of God's presence and power, manifesting the fruit and gifts of the Spirit.

We don't need to wait for heaven to plunge into the eternal river of life. Jesus has provided this blessing for us right now!

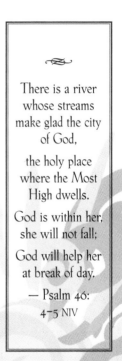

There is a river whose streams make glad the city of God,

the holy place where the Most High dwells.

God is within her, she will not fall;

God will help her at break of day.

— Psalm 46: 4–5 NIV

Let the rivers of living water flow through every area of your life today.

ears Turned to Joy

Many people know that the shortest verse in the Bible has only two words and nine letters: "Jesus wept" (John 11:35 KJV). But few know that there is another verse that also has only two words, although it is not the shortest verse because it has fifteen letters: "Rejoice evermore" (1 Thessalonians 5:16 KJV).

Is there a connection between these two verses? Most certainly!

Jesus wept at the tomb of his friend Lazarus, who had been dead for four days. He felt sorrow that his friend had experienced sickness and death, that his friends Mary and Martha had been put through the grieving process, but also that no one at the tomb understood Him.

No one saw that He was the resurrection and the life, that death had no hold over Him.

Jesus knew that within moments, Lazarus would be alive again, raised from death, and that the joy of His friends and disciples would be unbridled and ecstatic. But that knowledge did not keep Him from empathizing with the pain of His friends. Jesus weeps with us when bad things happen. He does not stand afar off, aloof, and disinterested. He feels what we feel. He hurts for us when we hurt.

But Jesus also knows something about our problem or crisis that we often do not know. He knows that the time is very near when our sorrow will end, our suffering will cease, and we will experience the great joy of the truly abundant life He bought for us at Calvary.

It is good for us to recognize that Jesus weeps when we weep. It is also right for us to move from our weeping into rejoicing as a sign of our faith in Jesus, faith that He cares deeply for us and will deliver us from sorrow.

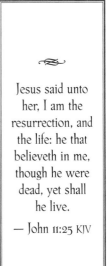

Jesus said unto her, I am the resurrection, and the life: he that believeth in me, though he were dead, yet shall he live.

— John 11:25 KJV

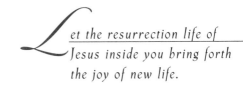

Let the resurrection life of Jesus inside you bring forth the joy of new life.

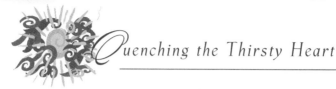

Quenching the Thirsty Heart

Brian Major's job as administrator for a major manufacturing company gave him the responsibility to make decisions with nationwide impact on the employees of his corporation. Over time, he noticed that his own ego was being exalted beyond measure and that his attitude toward other people was becoming cold and impersonal. Brian knew he was developing a hardened, insensitive heart, and even though he didn't want to have such a heart, he seemed incapable of changing on his own. His attempts at what he called "shallow prayer and mechanical Scripture reading" didn't work.

Then Brian began to listen to praise tapes in hopes that they might be for him the river of life that could quench his parched and dry soul. The more he listened to the praise and worship music, the more he experienced a softening of his heart, which was manifested in very specific ways.

Brian first noticed a new inclination to cry tears when he felt the Spirit of the Lord moving in his life — something he had not experienced in a long time. He had a less cynical attitude about God's mercy and a deep conviction regarding the harshness of his attitude toward some of his colleagues. He also had a desire to turn from his autocratic and traditional management style and become a more sensitive and responsive leader of the people he supervised.

The more Brian listened to praise music, the more he *desired* to listen to it. Even though he listened to some tapes dozens of times, the music lost none of its ability to melt his heart. Brian found that the "river of praise" that seemed to flow from his tape deck is now resident deep within him, where it continues to flow regardless of where he is or what he is doing.

Based upon a testimonial letter.

O Lord, the hope of Israel, all that forsake thee shall be ashamed... because they have forsaken the Lord, the fountain of living waters. Heal me, O Lord, and I shall be healed; save me, and I shall be saved: for thou art my praise.

— Jeremiah 17:13–14 KJV

Will you allow the Spirit to soften the hardened parts of YOUR heart today?

Revelation in Suffering

One of the last of the Scottish martyrs spoke about the persecution he experienced for years before he was put to death. On several occasions, he was put out of his home and forced to endure the harsh elements of the Scottish moors. He said:

> Enemies think themselves satisfied that we are put out to wander in mosses and upon mountains. But even amidst the storms of these last two nights, I cannot express what sweet times I have had when I had no covering but the dark curtains of night. In the silent watch, my mind was led out to admire the deep and inexpressible ocean of joy wherein the whole family of heaven swims. Each star led me to wonder what He must be who is the star of Jacob, of whom all stars borrow their shining.

When our souls are thirsty, we can choose to focus on our thirst or upon the One who satisfies our thirst. We can choose to focus on the darkness of the night or on the stars shining in the velvet sky. We can choose to feel persecuted or to feel blessed that we are counted worthy of standing boldly for such a magnificent Savior and Lord.

The more we wonder at the mercy and love of Jesus Christ — truly standing in awe and wonderment at His great provision for us — the more safe and secure and strong we will be in our future with Him.

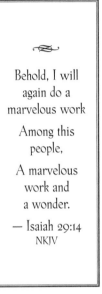

Behold, I will again do a marvelous work

Among this people,

A marvelous work and a wonder.

— Isaiah 29:14
NKJV

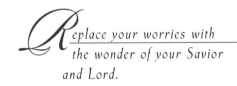

Replace your worries with the wonder of your Savior and Lord.

Heal Me, O Lord

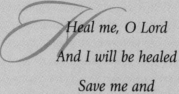

Heal me, O Lord
And I will be healed
Save me and
I will be saved

Heal me, O Lord

And I will be healed

For You are the One I praise

You are the One I praise 𝄞

Lyrics: Jeremiah 17:14 NIV
Music: Don Moen
© 1995 Integrity's Hosanna! Music

God Desires to Heal

When we meditate on passages of Scripture where Jesus healed people, He is literally becoming healing to us. He has the same compassion for us, and He is asking us the same question He has always asked, "Do you want Me to make you whole?"

Jesus was going about all the cities and the villages, teaching in their synagogues, and proclaiming the gospel of the kingdom, and healing every kind of disease and every kind of sickness. And seeing the multitudes, He felt compassion for them, because they were distressed and downcast.

— Matthew 9:35-36 NASB

And a leper came to Him, beseeching Him and falling on his knees before Him, and saying to Him, "If You are willing, You can make me clean." And moved with compassion, He stretched out His hand, and touched him, and said to him, "I am willing; be cleansed." And immediately the leprosy left him and he was cleansed.

— Mark 1:40-42 NASB

Jesus went along by the Sea of Galilee, and having gone up to the mountain, He was sitting there. And great multitudes came to Him, bringing with them those who were lame, crippled, blind, dumb, and many others, and they laid them down at His feet; and He healed them, so that the multitude marveled as they saw the dumb speaking, the crippled restored, and the lame walking, and the blind seeing; and they glorified the God of Israel.

— Matthew 15:29-31 NASB

And a certain man was there, who had been thirty-eight years in his sickness. When Jesus saw him lying there, and knew that he had already been a long time in that condition, He said to him, "Do you wish to get well." The sick man answered Him, "Sir, I have no man to put me into the pool when the water is stirred up, but while I am coming, another steps down before me." Jesus said to him, "Arise, take up your pallet, and walk." And immediately the man became well, and took up his pallet and began to walk.

— John 5:5-9 NASB

> Jesus Christ the same yesterday, and to day, and for ever.
>
> Hebrews 13:8 KJV

Healing is for today because Jesus is for today.

Healing Power

When Darlene Montgomery heard a praise tape about the healing power of God, she began to think, *God will do anything if I only ask Him.* She had a deep inner knowing that the Lord would heal her of lupus, from which she had suffered for years, and that He would do so in His timing and for His glory. She played that praise tape repeatedly until she had every word of it memorized. Its message of praise and healing literally became a part of her being.

A short while later at a prayer meeting, various people felt led to pray for Darlene. They didn't know she had been in great pain all month and was losing the use of her right arm. They simply were led of the Holy Spirit to have her come to a place in the room so everyone could anoint her with oil, lay hands on her, and pray for her healing. Immediately she felt the power of God and knew in her heart, *Now is the time.*

The Lord directed Darlene to pray healing scriptures for a week and to stand firm on His Word. She did so. When she went back to her doctor the next week, he could find no trace of lupus in her. All of her joints that had deteriorated were back to full strength and function. Her kidneys and bladder, which had slowly been shutting down, had returned to normal function. Her muscles were also showing signs of increased strength. The physician was amazed.

But the Lord wasn't finished doing His work in Darlene. About a month after she experienced physical healing, the Lord awoke her one night about 3:00 A.M. and spoke very clearly to her spirit, "Tell My people to pray Scripture. There is power in My Word." Darlene sensed a renewed purpose for her life. She since has spent countless hours encouraging others to read the Word, memorize the Word, say the Word aloud, and to sing God's Word. Her message is a simple but powerful one: "God's Word heals and restores."

Based on a testimonial letter.

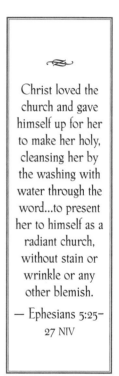

Christ loved the church and gave himself up for her to make her holy, cleansing her by the washing with water through the word...to present her to himself as a radiant church, without stain or wrinkle or any other blemish.

— Ephesians 5:25–27 NIV

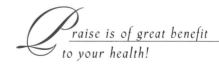

Praise is of great benefit to your health!

He Knows Everything

A little boy once asked his father, "Pa, does the Lord know everything?"

"Yes, my son," the father replied, "why do you ask?"

"Well, the preacher seems to pray so long, telling the Lord all kinds of things about the people he is praying for, I wasn't quite sure if the Lord was up on all the details."

Ask the Lord to heal you, but leave the details to Him. If you study the times Jesus healed people, you will see that each individual had a unique way to be healed. Some were touched by Jesus, while others just believed His Word. Some had to obey a command before they were healed. Still others were healed in the days following the moment Jesus prayed for them.

The Lord knows what we need more than we do. When we ask Him to make us whole, we can trust Him to know precisely when, where, and how to apply His healing power. The healing timetable He has for another person, He may not have for us. He knows precisely when we will be best able to receive the benefits He is sending our way. And the healing method He has for another person may not be the method He has for us. He has a one-of-a-kind remedy for us because we are a one-of-a-kind person.

He knows what needs immediate attention.

153

He knows what needs emergency techniques.

He knows what needs rehabilitation and long-term care.

He knows what needs a therapeutic daily remedy and what needs a one-time readjustment of priorities and attitudes.

He knows what needs to be vaccinated against and inoculated for.

He knows!

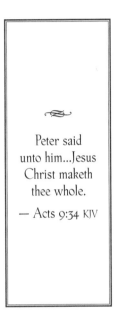

Peter said unto him...Jesus Christ maketh thee whole.

— Acts 9:34 KJV

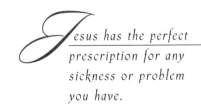

esus has the perfect prescription for any sickness or problem you have.

No Problem Too Big

After noted Princeton astronomer Henry Norris Russell had concluded a lecture on the Milky Way, a woman came to him and asked, "If our world is so little, and the universe is so great, how can we believe that God pays any attention to us?"

Dr. Russell replied, "That depends, madam, entirely on how big a God you believe in."

Do you have trouble believing that God can and does take notice of your need for healing? Do you believe that in the vast universe of problems, God is concerned about what ails, diminishes, or incapacitates *you*? Perhaps you need a bigger vision of God. Perhaps you need a renewed outlook on what it truly means for

God to be omnipotent (all-powerful), omniscient (all-knowing), and omnipresent (always present). What all these big words mean is that God is love.

A man came to Jesus one day seeking healing for his boy, who suffered from horrible convulsions and often fell to the ground writhing and foaming at the mouth. The man said, "Have mercy on us and do something if you can."

Jesus responded, "If I can? *Anything is possible if you have faith."*

To that the father instantly replied, "I *do* have faith; oh, help me to have *more!"* (See Mark 9:21-24 TLB.)

If your faith for healing seems weak and ineffective, if you have trouble believing that God could truly care about you or desire to heal you, ask Him to enlarge your vision and your faith. Ask Him to help you see Him as your willing and compassionate Healer. Ask Him to give you greater faith to believe that He not only can, but will deliver you.

> [Jesus said], "If you had faith even as small as a tiny mustard seed you could say to this mountain, 'Move!' and it would go far away. Nothing would be impossible."
>
> — Matthew 17:20 TLB

God eclipses your biggest need by His transforming power.

God's Healing Methods

One afternoon while playing on a wooden picnic table, a little boy ran a splinter into his finger. Sobbing, he called his father, who was a pastor, at his office. He said, "Daddy, I want God to take the splinter out."

The father said, "Go to your mother. She'll be able to remove it for you."

"No," the little boy insisted. "I want *God* to take it out."

"Why don't you trust your mother to do this?" his father asked.

"Because when Mommy takes a splinter out, it hurts. If God takes it out by Himself, it won't hurt."

When the father arrived home at the end of his workday, he found his son still nursing a sore and inflamed finger. In spite of his son's initial protests, the father proceeded to remove the splinter. The procedure was a bit painful, but the relief was complete.

Two truths about healing stand out in this little story:

First, God sometimes involves others in our healing process. He uses people to bring healing to others — His methods include the work of physicians, counselors, and those who pray. Avail yourself of all the help God is making available to you. Ask Him to lead you to precisely the right people who will help you best and build you up in wholeness — body, mind, and spirit.

Second, the healing process is sometimes a little painful. That pain is nearly always temporary. The physical therapist may require movement that results in sore muscles. Incisions may be painful in the aftermath of surgery. The counseling process may uncover old wounds that need to be lanced emotionally so that they can heal properly. We often must be willing to undergo short-term discomfort to get a result that is eternally peaceful, joyous, comforting, and results in our wholeness. The good news is that once a person is healed, the pain that was part of the process passes and is generally forgotten.

Look for God's healing hand in everyone and everything He sends your way.

> As He passed by, He saw a man blind from birth...He spat on the ground, and made clay of the spittle, and applied the clay to his eyes, and said to him, "Go, wash in the pool of Siloam"...so he went away and washed, and came back seeing.
>
> — John 9:1,6–7
> NASB

God has unlimited methods for healing.

A Choice that Alters History

Before William Booth became a full-time minister, he conducted religious services as a lay preacher in small rural churches. At seventeen, he was made a preacher in the Methodist Church. His superintendent wanted him to become a full-time preacher at the age of nineteen, but Booth's doctor advised him against the ministry. He told Booth that his health was so poor that he was totally unfit for the strain of being a preacher!

Nevertheless, Booth undertook a ministry among London's poorest people, engaging in strenuous labor and long hours. He launched an international organization now called the Salvation Army, which still ministers the Gospel to the poor today. Booth lived to be eighty-three before he went home to be with the Lord.

When someone has M.D. behind their name, it means they are in the business of medical *practice*. A doctor's diagnosis is always limited, and the physician's prognosis is always clouded by human judgment. Only God knows what lies ahead for you and what you are capable of accomplishing. Whenever sickness and disease present themselves to you, listen to what the Holy Spirit tells you.

Booth chose to believe what Almighty God was speaking in his heart more than the negative and limiting report given to him by a human being. Consider what he would have missed had he built his life around man's words instead of what God had placed in his heart. History is filled with men, women, and children who have trusted in the supernatural healing power of God to overcome natural odds and achieve great things for the kingdom of God.

> Now faith is the substance of things hoped for, the evidence of things not seen.
>
> For by it the elders obtained a good report.
>
> Through faith we understand that the worlds were framed by the word of God, so that things which are seen were not made of things which do appear.
>
> — Hebrews 11:1-3 KJV

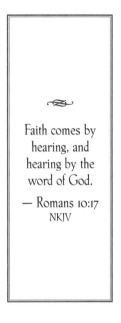

Faith comes by hearing, and hearing by the word of God.

— Romans 10:17 NKJV

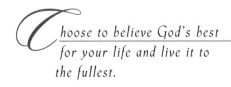

Choose to believe God's best for your life and live it to the fullest.

God Heals Broken Relationships

Kevin Wallace was devastated when he found himself separated eight months after his marriage. When he learned soon after that he had a daughter named Diana, he immediately went to see her, but was turned away. Brokenhearted, Kevin abided by his wife's wishes.

A year and a half later, Kevin learned that his wife wanted him to take Diana. He happily brought her home and showered her with love, but two days later, his wife returned and took Diana away. The separation led to a divorce, and his ex-wife moved to another state, *taking* Diana with her. Kevin lost all contact with his daughter.

Today Kevin has been married for more than thirty years to Miriam. He praises God for the healing of his heart and the birth of their three daughters, Madeline, Melinda, and Maureen. Still, all these years he prayed that God would restore his relationship with Diana.

One day a friend told Kevin that his former mother-in-law, who lived nearby, had died. When Kevin shared this news with his wife and daughters, Madeline began to think, *This was our sister's grandmother. Diana will no doubt be in town for the funeral.* Madeline wrote a letter to the half-sister she had never met and took it to the funeral home, asking that it be given to Diana.

Meanwhile, Diana had accepted Jesus as a young girl and was a devout Christian. As a young adult, she had a growing desire to see her father. When she married and had a son, one of her first thoughts was, *I want my little boy to know his grandpa.* She asked the Lord for a sign that she should get in touch with her father. Then she got the letter from Madeline.

Within two days, Diana had contacted the family and was soon united with them. Emotionally, they discussed the years that had passed, and both Diana and Kevin realized that their meeting and the emotional healing in each of their lives had been paved by the prayers of loving Christian friends. They each saw God make a way for them.

Based on a testimonial letter.

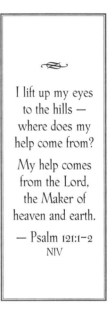

I lift up my eyes to the hills — where does my help come from?

My help comes from the Lord, the Maker of heaven and earth.

— Psalm 121:1–2
NIV

God is always at work for our good, even when His work is unseen.

arry Away a Song!

W hat do we do after we have expressed our need for healing and wholeness to the Lord?

> *Tell Him about the heartache,*
>
> *And tell Him the longings, too.*
>
> *Tell Him the baffled purpose*
>
> *When we scarce know what to do.*
>
> *Then leaving all our weakness*
>
> *With the One divinely strong,*
>
> *Forget that we bore a burden*
>
> *And carry away a song.[1]*

The Lord *will* answer our prayers — in His timing, by His method, and according to His purposes on this earth. We can trust Him to work for our eternal benefit and to fulfill His plan for us and others around us. The best response we can make after our own prayer for healing is to praise God for His answer and to leave all the details of His answer up to Him.

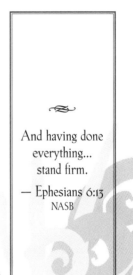

And having done everything... stand firm.

— Ephesians 6:13
NASB

Praise God for His lovingkindness toward you, for all He is doing in and through you.

God Will Make a Way

God will make a way

Where there seems to be no way

He works in ways we cannot see

He will make a way for me

He will be my guide

Hold me closely to His side

With love and strength for each new day

He will make a way He will make a way

By a roadway in the wilderness

He'll lead me

Rivers in the desert will I see

Heaven and earth will fade

But His Word will still remain

And He will do something new today ♪

Don Moen
© 1990 Integrity's Hosanna! Music

Even Where There Seems to Be No Way

Late one evening, Don Moen received a phone call with devastating news: his wife's sister had lost her oldest son in an automobile accident. Craig and Susan Phelps and their four sons were traveling through Texas on their way to Colorado when their van was struck broadside by an eighteen-wheeler truck. All four boys were thrown from the van.

Craig and Susan located their sons by their cries — one boy was lying in the ditch, another in an area wet from melted snow. Nearby was his brother who landed by a telephone pole. All were seriously injured, but when Craig, a medical doctor, reached Jeremy, he found him lying by a fence post with his neck broken. There was nothing Craig could do to revive him.

When Don received news of this tragedy a few hours later, he recalls, "My whole world came to a standstill, but I had to get on a plane the next morning and fly to a recording session that had been scheduled for several weeks. Although I knew Craig and Susan were hurting, I couldn't be with them until the day before the funeral.

"During the flight the morning after the accident, God gave me a song for them: 'God will make a way where there seems to be no way. He works in ways we cannot see. He will make a way for me.' The song was based upon Isaiah 43:19 NASB — 'Behold, I will do something new, now it will spring forth; will you not be aware of it? I will even make a roadway in the wilderness, rivers in the desert.'"

This song would bring comfort to Craig and Susan when all hope seemed lost. It touched the hurt in their hearts with hope and encouragement. Don received a letter from Susan in which she quoted Isaiah 43:4 NASB: "Since you are precious in My sight, since you are honored and I love you, I will give other men in your place and other peoples in exchange for your life."

Susan wrote, "We've seen the truth of that scripture." When Jeremy's friends learned that he had accepted Jesus into his life before he died, many of them began to ask their own parents how they could be assured of going to heaven when they died. The accident also prompted Craig and Susan into a deeper walk with the Lord as well as into new avenues of ministry. Craig began teaching Sunday school at their church and Susan became active in Women's Aglow, sharing with various groups her story and the Lord's provision in her time of sorrow.

She has since said, "The day of the accident, when I got out of the van, even before I knew our son was dead, I knew I had a choice. I could be bitter and angry or I could totally accept God and whatever He had for us. I had to make the decision that fast. I've seen fruit come as a result of that choice. If I had to, I'd do it again. It's worth it knowing others will go to heaven because of what happened to Jeremy. God really did make a way for us!"

Soon after "God Will Make a Way" was recorded, people from around the world began to write and call, sharing with Don how they had experienced similar tragedies. All of the calls and letters had one great theme — God had made a way for them when all hope seemed to be lost! God had carried them through a shattering situation, and by His grace, they were emerging with stronger faith, renewed hope, and increased courage on the other side of heartache and loss.

The truth of God's Word is always that He will make a way for those who rely solely upon Him. The exact path is of His choosing. The exact methods are of His design, but He will bring us through to greater wholeness every time we place our trust in Him.

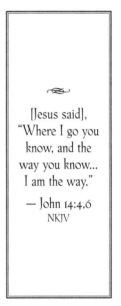

[Jesus said],
"Where I go you
know, and the
way you know...
I am the way."

— John 14:4,6
NKJV

*Stay close to Jesus and
you'll always find a way.*

A Path Where None Existed

Could any night have seemed so dark to Moses? Pharaoh had relented and said, "Go," but now he and the tens of thousands of Hebrew families who had traveled with him, along with their flocks and herds, found themselves facing the Red Sea. They camped in a spot precisely chosen by God, and Moses wondered, *Did I hear God correctly?* There was no way across the sea here. The waters were deep, wide, and swiftly flowing.

They could not move forward; neither could they turn back. Pharaoh had sent an army of six hundred chariots and horses to force them to return to their slave quarters. The army had arrived on the scene and was camped just beyond a nearby hill. Nevertheless, throughout the long night, the light of God's presence filled the camp of the Israelites. Strangely, the Egyptians made no move to disturb them. Although they were camped nearby, they seemed blinded by the very light that illumined the Israelite camp.

And then God's command came, "Moses, take your rod in your hand and stretch out your hand over the sea." Moses rose to obey, and as he did what God commanded, the waters of the Red Sea began to move. All that night, a strong east wind drove a wedge into the sea, pushing the waters to the north and south, making the ground on the bottom of the sea hard and dry.

A path now beckoned where none had ever existed! Moses led his people on that path, with great walls of water on the right and left. They continued moving forward until they finally reached the other side of the sea. God had made a path where none existed before!

What is God telling you to do? What truth of His love, forgiveness, and healing power is He whispering on the winds of the Spirit as He calls out to your soul? Today may very well be the day when the dark waters part. God is moving to make a way for you. Be ready to walk in it!

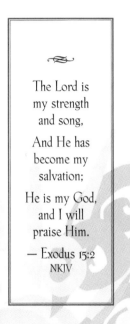

The Lord is my strength and song,

And He has become my salvation;

He is my God, and I will praise Him.

— Exodus 15:2
NKJV

Even when your back is to the wall, God has a way of escape.

Unlimited Options

Dwight L. Moody told the story of a boy who was brought up in an English orphanage. He had never learned to read or write, although he could recite the letters of the alphabet. One day a man came to him and told him that if he prayed to God in times of trouble, God would send help.

Shortly after this, the boy was apprenticed to a farmer. One day he was out tending the farmer's sheep and he was having a great deal of trouble keeping the flock together. He remembered what the man had said, so he decided to give prayer a try.

A passerby saw the boy on his knees near a hedge and overheard him praying, "A, B, C, D," and so on. The man asked, "Son, what are you doing?" The boy looked up and replied, "I'm praying."

"But you are reciting the alphabet," the man said. "That's not prayer."

The boy replied, "I don't know how to pray, sir, but a man once told me that if I called upon God, He would help me. So I thought that if I just named the letters of the alphabet, God could take them and put them together into the right prayer and give me what I need."

In the midst of our problems, we often do not know *how* to pray or precisely *what* to pray for. We are wise to say simply, "God, make a way," and then trust Him with all the details.

God has unlimited options and ways. Let Him choose the one that is right for you!

I have trusted in Your mercy.

— Psalm 13:5 NKJV

Walk in God's way instead of asking Him to do things your way.

Trusting the Way-Maker

He who dwells in the secret place of the Most High
Shall abide under the shadow of the Almighty.
I will say of the Lord, "He is my refuge and my fortress;
My God, in Him will I trust."

Surely He shall deliver you from the snare of the fowler
And from the perilous pestilence.
He shall cover you with His feathers,
And under His wings you shall take refuge;
His truth shall be your shield and buckler.
You shall not be afraid of the terror by night,
Nor of the arrow that flies by day,
Nor of the pestilence that walks in darkness,
Nor of the destruction that lays waste at noonday.

A thousand may fall at your side,
And ten thousand at your right hand;
But it shall not come near you.
Only with your eyes shall you look,
And see the reward of the wicked.

Because you have made the Lord, who is my refuge,
Even the Most High, your dwelling place,

No evil shall befall you,
Nor shall any plague come near your dwelling;
For He shall give His angels charge over you,
To keep you in all your ways.

— Psalm 91:1-11 NKJV

Too often we look for others to make a way for us when God is there all the time. We put our trust in a beloved family member, an employer, a government agency, a judge and jury, a friend, a pastor, when God is the Way-Maker. He alone knows the ending from the beginning of the path He desires for us to walk — and He alone promises to walk every step of the way with us.

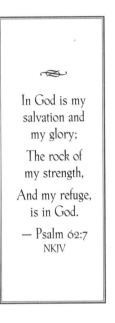

In God is my salvation and my glory;

The rock of my strength,

And my refuge, is in God.

— Psalm 62:7
NKJV

Meditate on Psalm 91 regularly and God will truly become your salvation in all matters.

Piercing the Heart

It was a Saturday morning in April when Sherry Stone finally decided to listen to the tape of "God Will Make a Way." Sherry stopped listening to music four years ago when her son, Paul, died. Something about a song reached deep down within her and caused her to feel the strong emotions of grief, sorrow, and loss that she was otherwise able to suppress. Music was so distressing to her that she even turned off the chimes on her mantel clock. The only music she could bear to hear was the music she helped make in her church choir. As long as Sherry was singing, she seemed to be in control of a song. But when she was listening, the song seemed to take control of her.

Then the choir leader at Sherry's church chose to do *God with Us* and asked each choir member to listen closely to the music before rehearsals began. Sherry had little recourse. She *had* to listen to the *God with Us* tape if she wanted to be part of the choir.

As Sherry sat alone in her home listening to the words and music of "God Will Make a Way," she felt God's presence very strongly. Tears began to flow, as though a dam broke inside her. A flood of tears erupted from the depths of her heart. She felt God speak to her spirit, "It's time to go on." Soon her tears gave way to the solid ground of faith in her Father God. A great feeling of peace engulfed her. At long last, the Holy Spirit healing had begun.

In the months that followed, Sherry was given several opportunities to speak to groups about what it means to lose a loved one and then find that God has made a way for life to continue. She also put together a six-week curriculum for support groups for those who are grieving a loss in their lives. Sherry had experienced how much it meant to be encouraged and to have hope restored. She now lives to share that message of encouragement and hope with others.

Based on a testimonial letter from Sherry Stone, who was part of the *God with Us* performance at Prestonwood Baptist Church in Dallas on June 23, 1993.

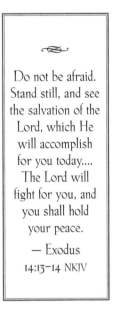

Do not be afraid. Stand still, and see the salvation of the Lord, which He will accomplish for you today.... The Lord will fight for you, and you shall hold your peace.

— Exodus 14:13–14 NKJV

When you allow the Holy Spirit to move in your heart, healing always comes.

One Step at a Time

One migration season, three whales captured the headlines of the world when they became entrapped in a rapidly forming ice flow. Would-be rescuers were stumped as to what they might do to free the whales from their captivity within the "fence of ice." The ice was forming rapidly around the whales, and soon scientists predicted there would be no way for the whales to surface and breathe the oxygen they needed to survive.

Finally one naturalist suggested that the whales might be lured to a breathing hole drilled just a few yards away, and then lured to yet another breathing hole even farther away. As new breathing holes were drilled, old ones were covered over, leaving the whales with no alternative — they had to move under the ice flow or die. Over the next several days, dozens of such breathing holes were drilled short distances apart to lead the whales step by step out of their problem and into the open waters.

The way God makes for us through a difficult time is often a step-by-step process. We must walk out the solution, step by step, day by day, decision by decision. It may seem that we take one step backward for every two steps forward, but if we could see the bigger picture of what God is doing, we would conclude, "Things *are* getting better."

Sometimes God delivers His children overnight, in a single, dramatic act.

But other times, a slow and gradual leading, requiring deliberate and steady obedience on our part, may be His way.

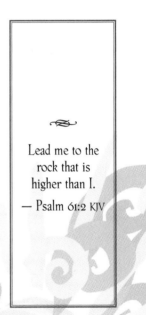

❧

Lead me to the
rock that is
higher than I.

— Psalm 61:2 KJV

To walk in the way God
provides, keep on your
walking shoes: faith
and obedience.

A Road in the Wilderness and Rivers in the Desert

In a genuine wilderness, there are no roads or even well-worn paths. This is especially true in the Middle East, where desert sands can shift overnight, completely changing the dunes and valleys of a landscape. A roadway in the wilderness must be revealed and pursued on a daily basis.

How do you navigate across shifting sands? By looking into the face of the clear night sky, getting one's bearings in relationship to the stars, and pursuing a course regardless of what things may look like the following morning. So it is with our lives. As we look to the Lord for guidance and direction, we know where to walk and what to do — regardless of the shifting circumstances around us.

And what about rivers in the desert? They do exist — they simply don't flow upon the surface of the sands where we can readily see them. Rather, water in the desert flows deep under the earth's crust. At times, it flows up through crevices of rock to form an artesian well or an oasis. Other times, it puddles just below the surface and a well must be dug. The river is always flowing, however, and if you dig deep enough, the water can be brought to the surface.

So it is with God's provision. It is always available, just under the surface of what we can see or experience. Occasionally God causes His provision to appear before us suddenly and effortlessly. Often, though, His provision is not so obvious, and we must dig deeper. The good news of God's provision is that He knows the way through the wilderness. He provides the life-giving water that we need on a daily basis. He is our guide and He will provide.

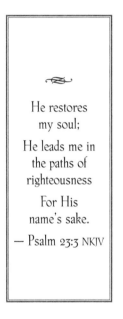

He restores
my soul;

He leads me in
the paths of
righteousness

For His
name's sake.

— Psalm 23:3 NKJV

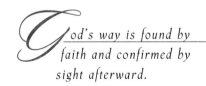

God's way is found by faith and confirmed by sight afterward.

It Is Well with My Soul

When peace like a river
Attendeth my way
When sorrows like
Sea billows roll
Whatever my lot
Thou hast taught me to say
It is well it is well
With my soul

It is well with my soul
It is well it is well
With my soul

Though Satan should buffet
Though trials should come
Let this blest
Assurance control

That Christ has regarded
My helpless estate
And hath shed His own blood
For my soul

And Lord haste the day
When the faith
Shall be sight
The clouds be rolled
Back as a scroll
The trump shall resound
And the Lord shall descend
Even so
It is well with my soul ♪

Horatio G. Spafford and Phillip Bliss
Public Domain

Yet Will I Praise Him

As a forty-three-year-old Chicago businessman, Horatio G. Spafford was suffering a heavy, two-fisted blow: the death of a son and financial disaster as the result of the Great Chicago Fire of 1871. Spafford determined that he and his family needed to get away from Chicago for a break from their heartache. Hearing that their friend Dwight L. Moody was going to preach a series of evangelistic crusades in England in the fall, Spafford decided that these meetings would be a good opportunity for spiritual, emotional, and physical renewal for his family. He and his wife began to make plans for the family to go to England. Spafford sent his wife and four daughters ahead of him on the SS

Ville du Havre while he completed some business obligations in America. He intended to follow them a few days later.

On the Atlantic crossing, the SS Ville du Havre was struck by an iron sailing vessel and it sank within twelve minutes. Two hundred and twenty-six lives were lost, including the Spaffords' four daughters. When the survivors were brought to shore at Cardiff, Wales, Mrs. Spafford sent this cablegram to her husband: "Saved alone."

Spafford immediately booked passage on the next ship. As he was crossing the Atlantic, the captain pointed out the place where he estimated the SS Ville du Havre had gone down. That night in his cabin, in his deep grief and knowing that he was crossing over the watery graves of his beloved girls, Spafford penned the words, "When sorrows like sea billows roll; whatever my lot, Thou hast taught me to say, 'It is well, it is well with my soul.'"[1]

Our abiding hope as Christians is that the day will come when we will be with our Lord and our loved ones in a peaceful, joyous reunion. In the interim, no matter what happens to us, we must let our heavenly Father turn our ashes to beauty and our sorrows to joy.

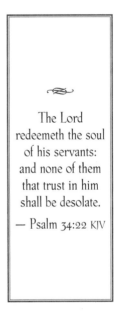

The Lord redeemeth the soul of his servants: and none of them that trust in him shall be desolate.

— Psalm 34:22 KJV

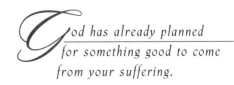

God has already planned for something good to come from your suffering.

The Genuine Mark of Confidence

To say, "It is well with my soul" is not a sign of resignation. Nor is it a build-up-yourself statement about self-esteem. It is the mark of confidence that God is God and He is present with you. Genuine well-being of soul is knowing with absolute certainty that you are forgiven and in a fully-reconciled relationship with God the Creator. It is knowing beyond any shadow of a doubt that Jesus Christ is your Lord and the Holy Spirit abides within your heart. It is knowing that having such a relationship with God the Father, God the Son, and God the Holy Spirit is the only thing that truly matters in this life.

Years ago, St. Teresa wrote about the confidence we can have in God:

> Let nothing disturb thee,
> Nothing affright thee;
> All things are passing;
> God never changeth;
> Patient endurance
> Attaineth to all things.
> Whom God possesseth
> In nothing is wanting:
> Alone God sufficeth.[2]

Even if we lose everything, if we know the Lord, we have all that we need.

Even if every other person on earth abandons us in our hour of need, if we know the Lord, we have all that is necessary for love.

Even if all of our computers and knowledge fail us, if we know the

Lord, we have all that we need for understanding and peace of mind.

Even if all of our talents and abilities seem to vanish, if we know the Lord, we have all that we need to live an effective, productive, meaningful, and satisfying life.

If we know the Lord, no matter what else may happen to us, we can know that our future is secure.

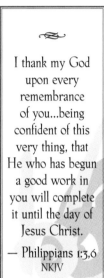

I thank my God upon every remembrance of you...being confident of this very thing, that He who has begun a good work in you will complete it until the day of Jesus Christ.

— Philippians 1:3,6
NKJV

To know the Lord is to know the One who knows everything there is to know.

Deliverance from Depression

Cindy Haynes slid into a severe depression when she started a new job. She felt she had made a terrible mistake in changing jobs, but that quitting her new job would only make matters worse. She eventually thought she was going crazy and wanted to die, so for three years she took medication and underwent therapy.

One day Cindy's friend Faye shared Jeremiah 29:11-14 with her. Almost immediately, those verses impacted her mind and heart. Again and again, the Lord brought to her mind that He *did* have a plan for her life. She even began to see that the job change was part of God's plan to bring her to a place where she would rely only upon Him.

Faye also introduced Cindy to the power of praise, giving her books on praise and worship and tapes of praise and worship music. One day as she was driving to work, Cindy was listening to a praise tape about God's power and His desire to heal. Suddenly she had a knowing in her heart that He was going to lift her out of the pit of depression and felt such a release in her spirit that she began to weep. She listened to the tape again and again. Then she began to listen to a tape that emphasized God's unconditional love. Again, she felt overwhelmed by the presence and power of His love for her.

Cindy's life changed abruptly. No longer did her thoughts dwell on failure, disappointment, and discouragement. Now her mind and heart focused on the glory and majesty of the Lord and her intimate relationship with Him. Again and again the Holy Spirit brought specific songs of praise to her mind at precisely the moments when she needed them most. Rather than need medications, she found herself needing only Jesus.

Praising Jesus became Cindy's true occupation! Her job was merely her way of earning money. Says Cindy, "Lifting my praise to God helped me release my love for and to Him in a way I had never been able to express."

Based upon a testimonial letter from Cindy Haynes.

Be at rest once more, O my soul, for the Lord has been good to you.

— Psalm 116:7 NIV

As we lift our praises to God, our spirits are lifted.

A Prayer for Peace

One of the most famous prayers for the well-being of a soul was prayed by St. Francis of Assisi:

Lord, make me a channel of thy peace

That where there is hatred I may bring love,

That where there is wrong I may bring the spirit of forgiveness,

That where there is discord I may bring harmony,

That where there is error I may bring truth,

That where there is doubt I may bring faith,

That where there is despair I may bring hope,

That where there were shadows I may bring thy light,

That where there is sadness I may bring joy.

Lord, grant that I may seek rather

To comfort — than to be comforted;

To understand — than to be understood;

To love — than to be loved;

For it is by giving that one receives;

It is by self-forgetting that one finds;

It is by forgiving that one is forgiven;

It is by dying that one awakens to eternal life.[3]

If you are in need of peace today, become a channel for the peace of God to someone else. If you are in need of a sense of confidence and well-being in your soul, seek to help someone else to be more confident in the grace of God. What you give is what God will multiply back to you in the very way you need it most.

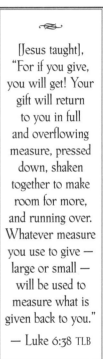

[Jesus taught], "For if you give, you will get! Your gift will return to you in full and overflowing measure, pressed down, shaken together to make room for more, and running over. Whatever measure you use to give — large or small — will be used to measure what is given back to you."

— Luke 6:38 TLB

When we turn ourselves inside out for others, the world around us often turns right side up.

An End Will Come

As William Dean Howells and Mark Twain were leaving church one Sunday morning, the heavens opened up and the area was drenched with a heavy rain.

"Do you think it will stop?" asked Howells.

"It always has," answered Twain.[4]

This is a humorous anecdote, but it reveals a great truth: No matter how long, fierce, or dark a time of sorrow or trouble may be, the end of it *will* come. No crisis lasts forever. It is eventually resolved in some way, by some means. This is true in every area of our lives.

When we experience a crisis, our initial reaction is something akin to some of the more primitive peoples in the world. They believe that whatever is happening in the present is their fate forever. For example, if you put one of these tribesmen in jail, they will stop eating and drinking because they believe they will be there forever. They have no will to live behind bars their entire life, so they seek death to escape.

When our crisis comes, we often lose sleep and appetite. We are agitated and begin to think of all the terrible outcomes for the disaster we are facing. However, the Bible clearly tells us we are to do things differently. When hit with a crisis, we are to immediately walk boldly into the throne room of our Father God and obtain mercy and grace in our time of need. (See Hebrews 4:16.) We are to trust God for deliverance.

We can actually hasten the end of the dark time by entering the light of God's presence in prayer and seeking wisdom from His Word. Then, as we sing praises to Him, our prison doors will open just as they did for Paul and Silas. He will restore our wounded souls with His peace and give us joy and strength to continue on the path He has set for us.

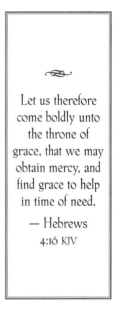

Let us therefore come boldly unto the throne of grace, that we may obtain mercy, and find grace to help in time of need.

— Hebrews 4:16 KJV

Meet the challenge of a crisis with God's Word, prayer, and praise to Him.

Soul Peace

When Mrs. Groves received word that her mother had cancer in a fairly advanced stage, she was devastated. Her mother was a good churchgoer, but Mrs. Groves had no peace in her heart that her mother had ever surrendered her life to the Lord. She wanted to be certain her mother was born again.

As she began to pray for her mother, the Lord quickened Isaiah 42:16 NASB to her: "I will lead the blind by a way they do not know, in paths they do not know I will guide them. I will make darkness into light before them and rugged places into plains. These are the things I will do, and I will not leave them undone." The Lord also encouraged Mrs. Groves that praise would be her own key to survival during this difficult time.

A few weeks later, as Mrs. Groves and her eighteen-year-old daughter drove to be with her mother, they listened to praise tapes almost every minute of their thousand-mile journey. By the time they arrived, they both felt they had a reservoir of strength for the situation they faced.

Within a week, Mrs. Groves' sweet eighty-five-year-old mother had prayed with Mrs. Grove's daughter to receive the Lord! She went home to be with Jesus ten days later. Mrs. Groves wrote, "It is difficult to grieve because I am so thrilled at her salvation."

There is no peace like the peace of mind that comes when we truly know we are saved. It is only after we have accepted God's forgiveness and have yielded ourselves completely to His will for us that we can proclaim, "It is WELL with my soul."

Based on a testimonial letter from Dr. and Mrs. Berton Groves.

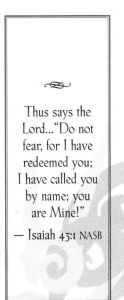

Thus says the Lord..."Do not fear, for I have redeemed you; I have called you by name; you are Mine!"

— Isaiah 43:1 NASB

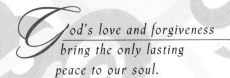

God's love and forgiveness bring the only lasting peace to our soul.

Believe for the Fog to Lift

George Mueller was a powerful man of faith. He received more than two million dollars to fund the orphanages he founded without ever advertising or soliciting funds. Every penny came as an answer to prayer.

On a trip from England to Quebec, the ship on which Mueller was traveling hit a heavy bank of fog. Mueller found the captain and said, "Captain, I have come to tell you I must be in Quebec on Saturday afternoon."

The captain said, "That is impossible."

Mueller replied, "Then very well, if your ship cannot take me, God will find some other way. I have never broken an engagement in fifty-seven years; let us go down into the chart room and pray."

The captain said, "Do you know how dense this fog is?"

"No," Mueller said, "my eye is not on the density of the fog, but on the living God who controls every circumstance of my life." Mueller then knelt down and prayed a simple prayer. When he finished, the captain began to speak, but Mueller put his hand on his shoulder and told him not to pray.

"As you do not believe He will answer, and as I believe He has, there is no need whatsoever for you to pray about it. I have known my Lord for fifty-seven years and there has never been a single day when I have failed to get an audience with the King. Get up, Captain, and open the door and you will find the fog has gone."

The captain arose, opened the door, and discovered that the fog had lifted. George Mueller kept his promised engagement on Saturday afternoon in Quebec.[5]

Regardless of precisely how and when God answers our prayers, He always responds to the prayer of faith. Trust Him today and all will be well with you.

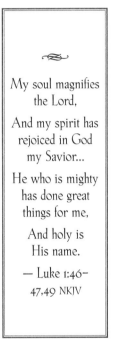

My soul magnifies the Lord,

And my spirit has rejoiced in God my Savior...

He who is mighty has done great things for me,

And holy is His name.

— Luke 1:46–47,49 NKJV

No matter how dense the fog may be today, the SON *is shining above it.*

Look Around!

When the King of Syria received word that the prophet Elisha was in Dothan, he immediately sent a great army to take the prophet captive. The army completely surrounded the city with its horses and chariots. Elisha's servant arose early the next morning and went out onto the city wall. When he saw the army encamped below, he came to Elisha, crying, "Alas, my master! What shall we do?"

Elisha answered, "Do not fear, for those who are with us are more than those who are with them." Then he prayed for his servant, "Lord, I pray, open his eyes that he may see." The Lord opened the eyes of the young man, and when he looked again at the scene before him, he saw something entirely different. The mountains surrounding them were filled with horses and chariots of fire! Indeed, those who were with Elisha far outnumbered those who were against him. Not only were they greater in number, but they were greater in power. (See 2 Kings 6:8-17.)

What gives us confidence and well-being when we are under attack from the enemy is catching a glimpse of the great warriors who stand ready to engage in battle on our behalf. Whether we have just lost a loved one, are trying to dig our way out of heavy debt, or we are battling a disease, we must remember that God has put all the resources of heaven at our disposal.

Through the blood of Jesus and by His name, we have authority over all the power of the enemy. Like Jesus, when the enemy comes to tempt us or try us, we have God's Word to defeat him and send him packing. And the Bible says that when we speak God's Word over our situation, the angels are dispatched to perform the Word of God in our lives. Peace of mind and heart is knowing that all of heaven is on our side while we are on this earth.

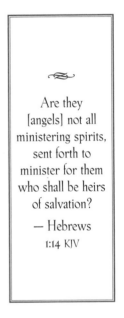

Are they [angels] not all ministering spirits, sent forth to minister for them who shall be heirs of salvation?

— Hebrews
1:14 KJV

When the storms of life get you down, open your spiritual eyes and see God at work.

Be Still My Soul

Be still my soul, be still my soul
Cease from the labor and the toil
Refreshing springs of peace await
To troubled minds and hearts that ache

Be still my soul, God knows your way
And He will guide for His name's sake
Plunge in the rivers of His grace
Rest in the arms of His embrace

Be still my soul, be still my soul

Though battles 'round you rage and roar

One thing you need and nothing more

To hear the whisper of your Lord

Be still my child, I know your way

And I will guide for My name's sake

Plunge in the rivers of My grace

Rest in the arms of My embrace ♪

Kim Noblitt
@1997 Integrity Praise! Music

A Fresh Look at Psalm 23

S ometimes we can become so familiar with a passage of Scripture that we
lose sight of the meaning. Read this familiar psalm from a new version
and let it speak to you in a whole new way.

God, my shepherd!
I don't need a thing.
You have bedded me down in lush meadows,
you find me quiet pools to drink from.
True to your word,
you let me catch my breath
and send me in the right direction.

Even when the way goes through
Death Valley,
I'm not afraid
when you walk at my side.
Your trusty shepherd's crook
makes me feel secure.

You serve me a six-course dinner
right in front of my enemies.
You revive my drooping head;
my cup brims with blessing.

Your beauty and love chase after me
every day of my life.
I'm back home in the house of God
for the rest of my life.

—Psalm 23
THE MESSAGE

He shall feed his
flock like a
shepherd: he shall
gather the lambs
with his arm, and
carry them in
his bosom, and
shall gently lead
those that are
with young.

—Isaiah 40:11 KJV

*The Lord is always there
to lead you and comfort
you.*

A Prayer of Compassion

At times when we are struggling or discouraged, we lose sight of a very simple fact: The Lord cares for us. He not only loves us with an infinite and unconditional love, but He cares what happens to us. He cares about what we feel and what we need. He often calls us to pray for others or others to pray for us — as in the prayer below. Someone may be praying just such a prayer for you today!

I said a prayer for you today
And know God must have heard
I felt the answer in my heart
Although He spoke not a word.
I didn't ask for wealth or fame
(I knew you wouldn't mind)
I asked for priceless treasures rare
Of a more lasting kind.

I prayed that He'd be near to you
At the start of each new day,
To grant you health and blessing fair,
And friends to share your way.

I asked for happiness for you
In all things great and small,
But that you'd know His loving care,
I prayed the most of all.[1]

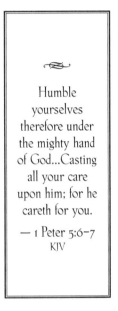

Humble
yourselves
therefore under
the mighty hand
of God...Casting
all your care
upon him; for he
careth for you.

— 1 Peter 5:6–7
KJV

*Humility is simply
following God's still
small voice in awe.*

Knowing the Shepherd's Voice

A man who had lived in the Middle East for quite some time and was very well acquainted with the shepherds in the nearby hills was out riding his horse one day when he came to a spring of water. He stopped to rest and shortly, a shepherd came down a steep mountain path near him, his flock of sheep following behind. Not long after, another shepherd with another flock came down to the water by another path, and after awhile a third. The three flocks mingled together, so that the man began to wonder how each shepherd was ever going to find his own sheep again.

At last one of the shepherds arose and called, "Men-ah!" — which is Arabic for "follow" — and his sheep came out from the larger flock and followed him back into the mountains. The man noticed that the shepherd didn't even turn around to count those that followed. Then the second shepherd got up and called out to his sheep, "Men-ah!" and those that belonged to his flock left the others and followed him back up the path.

The man was intrigued by what he saw and he said to the third shepherd, "I think I could make your sheep follow me."

"I doubt it," the shepherd replied.

"Give me your turban, your cloak, and your crook," the man challenged, "and we'll see." He put on the shepherd's clothing, took the crook in his hand, stood up where the sheep could see him, and called out in his best Arabic, "Men-ah! Men-ah!" Not one sheep took any notice of him.

The man asked the shepherd if the sheep ever followed anybody but him. The shepherd replied, "The only time a sheep will make a mistake and follow a stranger is when it gets sick."[2]

It is only when we become sick with sin in our souls that we fall prey to the enemy's call. As long as we are following the voice of the Lord, we are safe and blessed.

> [Jesus said], "My sheep hear My voice, and I know them, and they follow Me. And I give them eternal life, and they shall never perish; neither shall anyone snatch them out of My hand.
>
> — John 10:27–28 NKJV

Follow the voice of Jesus at all times. He will never lead you astray.

An Unusual Green Pasture

Several years ago, Diana Furey was flown to a Christian hospital in another state to be treated for an eating disorder and severe depression. Not wanting to be hospitalized, she agreed only because she was under threat of a court order. For seven weeks, she was separated from her three young children and her husband. She felt alone, frightened, and very angry at God.

It was during those seemingly endless weeks of hospitalization, however, that Diana began to understand the great depth of God's unconditional love for her, and a deep inner healing took place. Slowly, she began to see that even in the darkest moments of her life,

Jesus had always been with her. He had always been her Good Shepherd, but she had refused to receive His love and care.

As Diana yielded more and more of her life to Jesus, His love and peace replaced her anger and feelings of helplessness. Her self-destructive attitudes and the pain over tragedies in her past began to dissolve. She left the hospital confident that Jesus is greater than any circumstance she will ever face and that God will always be present to make a way for her. She wrote, "I stand before you healed by the grace of God."

At times we need to reach the end of ourselves before we are willing to accept the simple truth of the Gospel: The Lord is our Shepherd, and we are His sheep. We have no ability to rule our own lives, and thus, we have very little success in trying to do so. We cannot make wise decisions apart from His wisdom. We cannot even love ourselves as well as He loves us! With the Lord, however, we can do all things — and do them for His glory and our eternal reward.

Based upon a testimonial letter from Diana M. Furey.

> Oh, the depth of the riches both of the wisdom and knowledge of God! How unsearchable are His judgments and unfathomable His ways...For from Him and through Him and to Him are all things. To Him be the glory forever.
>
> — Romans 11:33,36
> NASB

Everybody follows someone or something. Make sure you are following Jesus.

The Lord Knows You by Name

Shepherds in the Middle East name their sheep. While an occasional lamb might be killed for a festive occasion, sheep are kept primarily for their wool. Shepherds develop a close and long-term relationship with the sheep under their care.

A man visiting the Middle East could not believe that sheep actually knew their own names, so he challenged a shepherd he met to call one or two of his sheep. The shepherd obliged and called out "Neriah." One of the sheep grazing nearby stopped eating and looked up. When the shepherd called out, "Come here," the sheep came immediately. He called another and another, and each did just as the first.

"But how can you tell them all apart?" the visitor asked. "To me, one looks just like the next."

The shepherd said, "Oh, no two are alike. Look closely. That sheep has lost a little bit of wool. That one is a little cross-eyed, this one is a little bowlegged, that one has a black spot on its nose." The visitor noted that the shepherd knew each of his sheep by their faults and failings. He didn't have a perfect sheep in his flock. Nevertheless, he cared for them and loved them equally.

How comforting to know that our heavenly Father sees us as we are and still loves us and cares for us. He knows each of us inside and out.

He delights in our uniqueness, including those qualities that still are being perfected! We are not "just another person with a need or a fault" to Him. We are His dear children, whom He is helping in every way He can to grow up and be like Jesus.

In all that we need, and all that we lack, may we turn to Him.

For all that He gives, and all that He calls us to do, may we thank Him.

With all that we are, and with all that we have, may we praise Him!

> The sheep hear his voice; and he calls his own sheep by name and leads them out. And when he brings out his own sheep, he goes before them; and the sheep follow him, for they know his voice.
>
> — John 10:3–4
> NKJV

Receive the tender love and care God has for you today.

Are You Listening?

A Bible translator was having difficulty finding a word for "obedience" in the native language of the people he was serving as a missionary. Obedience was a virtue that seldom seemed to be practiced among the people with whom he wanted to share the Gospel. Then one day as he was returning home, he whistled for his dog and it came running to him at full speed. An old native, observing the dog's quick reaction, said admiringly in the native tongue, "Your dog is all ear." The missionary knew immediately that he had his word for obedience.

Are you "all ear" to the Good Shepherd today? Are you listening intently for the command Jesus will give that will be the way out of your present difficulty? Are you being attentive at all times, waiting for His instructions on how and when to go? Or are you being distracted by the things of this world, such as television, movies, video games, overwork, or spending too much time on a sport or hobby?

We are in danger of missing God's way out of any period of distress or danger if we fail to be "all ears" to His Word and His Spirit. Being "all ears" means continuously listening for God's counsel and direction and then, when He tells us to do something, to do it immediately — no matter how strange it may be! If Naaman had only washed in the Jordan River six times, he would not have been healed.

The keys to God's deliverance include faith and obedience, and the keys to obedience are a willing heart and a listening ear.

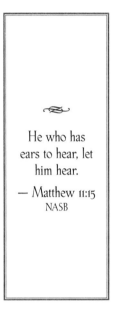

He who has ears to hear, let him hear.

— Matthew 11:15
NASB

What is the Lord whispering to your heart today?

*L*earning Obedience

King Henry III of Bavaria, like many of us today, was tired of his life and the pressures of his job. He was looking for a way "out." In search of something better, he made application to Prior Richard at a local monastery, asking to be accepted as a monk so he might spend the rest of his life in solitude and peace.

Prior Richard responded, "Your Majesty, do you understand that the pledge here is one of obedience? That will be hard because you have been a king."

Henry responded, "I understand. The rest of my life I will be obedient to you, as Jesus Christ leads you."

Prior Richard then said, "I will tell you what to do, then. Go back to your throne and serve faithfully in the place where God has put you."

After King Henry's death a number of years later, it was said of him: "The king learned to rule by being obedient."[3]

We often ask the Lord to remove us from our present circumstances and situations — and even relationships — in our desperation to be free of discomfort and difficulty. We are not unlike the apostle Paul, who begged the Lord to remove his "thorn in the flesh" three times. But the Lord answered that His grace was sufficient for Paul. (See 2 Corinthians 12:7-9.) He wanted him to discover the unlimited power of God's grace, and in order for that to happen, Paul had to be obedient beyond his natural abilities.

Our obedience to the Lord is based on unwavering faith. Our trust in Him and in His ability to work all things for our good must be rock-solid. When He directs us to stay in the job we are loathing or continue discipling a believer who is continuously backsliding we must allow His grace to be sufficient by obeying Him. When we obey, He is with us. And when He is with us, all is well and peace comes. We can do things we cannot do in our own strength and be wise beyond our natural ability.

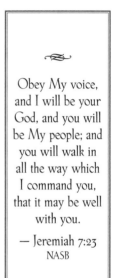

Obey My voice, and I will be your God, and you will be My people; and you will walk in all the way which I command you, that it may be well with you.

— Jeremiah 7:23
NASB

Obedience is learned in being willing to lie down in the pastures of God's choosing.

The Decision to Follow

God always makes a way for His people. The Bible gives us a great illustration of this in the lives of two men named Saul. They lived about a thousand years apart, but their lives have intriguing parallels.

One was a king; the other felt high honor in calling himself the servant of The King. One was a man who slew Philistines; the other was a champion of spiritual warfare. One started out well and ended poorly. The other started out poorly and ended well.

The first Saul gained a kingdom and a crown during his life. He had a loving family and a highly devoted son named Jonathan. He had a friendship with Samuel, the prophet and judge of Israel. In the end, Saul lost his crown, his kingdom, his son, his friendship with Samuel, his peace of heart, and his life. Why? He disobeyed the word of the Lord.

The second Saul was born a Jew with Roman citizenship and became a zealot for traditional Jewish practices. He led an effort to wipe out the early Church. Nevertheless, in the end he did more for the expansion of the Church and the spreading of the Gospel than any other person of that era. He wrote much of the New Testament, founded churches, and encouraged the spiritual growth of people in countless locations. Above all, he gained peace of heart and eternal life. What made the difference? He obeyed the word of the Lord.

But the key difference between these two men was not solely obedience, but love. King Saul of Israel loved himself more than God. The apostle Paul loved God more than himself. Have you made up your mind to love the Lord more than anyone or anything else? Have you yielded *all* to Him, so that no matter what He requires, and no matter what happens, you will follow Him? If you have done this, then great blessing awaits you, and whatever temptations, trials, and sorrow you face, He will be with you.

God will *always* make a way for you!

> [Jesus said], "If anyone serves Me, let him follow Me; and where I am, there My servant will be also. If anyone serves Me, him My Father will honor."
>
> — John 12:26 NKJV

Loving God is the most important priority in life, the key to fulfillment and joy.

Endnotes

1 He Will Come and Save You

[1] *Illustrations for Preaching and Teaching*, Craig Brian Larson, editor (Grand Rapids, MI: Baker Book House, 1993) p. 189–190.

[2] *The Treasure Chest* (San Francisco, CA: Harper, 1995) p. 121.

[3] *Encyclopedia of 7700 Illustrations*, Paul Lee Tan, editor (Dallas, TX: Bible Communications, 1979) p. 399.

[4] *The Treasure Chest* (San Francisco, CA: Harper, 1995) p. 171.

[5] *Encyclopedia of 7700 Illustrations*, Paul Lee Tan, editor (Dallas, TX: Bible Communications, 1979) p. 515.

[6] *Ibid.*, p. 512.

2 Cast Thy Burden

[1] *Encyclopedia of 7700 Illustrations*, Paul Lee Tan, editor (Dallas, TX: Bible Communications, 1979) p. 501-502.

[2] *Ibid.*, p. 523.

[3] *Illustrations for Preaching and Teaching*, Craig Brian Larson, editor (Grand Rapids, MI: Baker Book House, 1993) p. 19.

[4] *Encyclopedia of 7700 Illustrations*, Paul Lee Tan, editor (Dallas, TX: Bible Communications, 1979) p. 522.

[5] *Ibid.*, p. 1516.

3 Be Strong and Take Courage

[1] *Illustrations for Preaching and Teaching*, Craig Brian Larson, editor (Grand Rapids, MI: Baker Book House, 1993) p. 114.

[2] *Ibid.*, p. 176.

[3] *The Treasure Chest* (San Francisco, CA: Harper, 1995) p. 71.

[4] *Ibid.*

[5] *6000 Sermon Illustrations*, Elon Foster, editor (Grand Rapids, MI: Baker Book House, 1996) p. 145.

[6] *Encyclopedia of 7700 Illustrations*, Paul Lee Tan, editor (Dallas, TX: Bible Communications, 1979) p. 407.

4 No Eye Has Seen

[1] *Encyclopedia of 7700 Illustrations*, Paul Lee Tan, editor (Dallas, TX: Bible Communications, 1979) pp. 771–772.

[2] *Ibid.*, p. 1008.

[3] *Ibid.*

5   You Are Eternal

    [1] *1100 Illustrations from the Writings of D. L. Moody,* John W. Reed, editor (Grand Rapids, MI: Baker Book House, 1996) p. 18.

    [2] *The One Year Book of Hymns,* Robert K. Brown and Mark R. Norton, editors (Wheaton, IL: Tyndale House Publishers, 1995) July 8 entry.

    [3] *Illustrations for Preaching and Teaching,* Craig Brian Larson, editor ((Grand Rapids, MI: Baker Book House, 1993) p. 281.

6   All His Benefits

    [1] *1100 Illustrations from the Writings of D.L. Moody,* John W. Reed, editor (Grand Rapids, MI: Baker Book House, 1996) p. 124.

    [2] *Encyclopedia of 7700 Illustrations,* Paul Lee Tan, editor (Dallas, TX: Bible Communications, 1979) p. 277.

    [3] *Ibid.,* p. 479.

    [4] *1100 Illustrations from the Writings of D.L. Moody,* John W. Reed editor (Grand Rapids, MI: Baker Book House, 1996) p. 247.

    [5] *Encyclopedia of 7700 Illustrations,* Paul Lee Tan, editor (Dallas, TX: Bible Communications, 1979) p. 680.

8   Heal Me O Lord

    [1] *The Treasure Chest* (San Francisco, CA: Harper, 1995) p. 66.

10 It Is Well with My Soul

    [1] *The One Year Book of Hymns,* Robert Brown and Mark Norton, compilers (Wheaton, IL: Tyndale House Publishers, 1995) February 4 entry.

    [2] *The Treasure Chest* (SanFrancisco: Harper, 1995) p. 66.

    [3] *Ibid.,* p. 103.

    [4] *Encyclopedia of 7700 Illustrations,* Paul Lee Tan, editor (Dallas, TX: Bible Communications, 1979) p. 1359.

    [5] *Ibid.,* p. 404.

11 Be Still My Soul

    [1] *Resource Bimonthly,* Paul Lee Tan, editor (Dallas, TX: Bible Communications, 1979) entry R-123.

    [2] *1100 Illustrations from the Writings of D. L. Moody,* John W. Reed, editor (Grand Rapids, MI: Baker Book House, 1996) pp. 265-266.

    [3] *Illustrations for Preaching and Teaching,* Craig Brian Larson, editor (Grand Rapids, MI: Baker Book House, 1993) p. 166.

About Don Moen...

Between international and domestic tours and the daily demands of his full-time executive role, songwriter/artist/worship leader/business executive Don Moen often relaxes by donning his chef's apron to whip up a hearty breakfast for his family of seven or a skillet of rattlesnake chicken for staff meeting. Though he wears his near-celebrity status modestly, this dad of five is in constant demand as a worship leader throughout the world, in part due to his sensitive perspective on the joys and tragedies of life that touch us all. It is from those experiences and his close walk with the Lord that Don's creative energies flow. Out of the indescribable sorrow and pain at a close family member's death, Don was inspired to pen the words, "God will make a way, when there seems to be no way." His life and ministry are a testimony to that great truth.

After fifteen years of traveling worldwide as a musical missionary, Don Moen jointed Integrity Music in 1985. His heart and Integrity's mission melded together in a way that could only have been ordained by the Lord. Since that time Don has overseen the creation of hundreds of musical products, each focused on Integrity's stated mission of "Helping people worldwide experience the manifest presence of God, and develop a worship lifestyle." Integrity's products are now distributed in over 140 countries around the globe, and include thirteen which feature Don as worship leader. This *God Will Make a Way* devotional and the recording of the same title are a natural outgrowth of Integrity's ministry and Don's heart. We pray that through these words, songs, and testimonies, your life will be deeply touched by the Lord.

About Integrity...

Helping people worldwide experience the manifest presence of God...

This has been the mission of Integrity Incorporated since its founding in 1987. What began then as a mail order Christian Music Club has now grown into the world's largest independent Christian music company. As recipients of numerous nominations, awards, and 16 RIAA certified gold and platinum records, Integrity Incorporated now distributes its products in over 140 countries.

"We have experienced a phenomenal growth over the years," states Michael Coleman, President and CEO, "and we attribute this to God's hand guiding us to create resources that help His people experience His presence. Our commitment is to equip the Church worldwide in developing a worship lifestyle, and our products include local and international recordings as well as worship planning tools and choral products." With offices in the United States, the United Kingdom, Australia, and Singapore, Integrity Incorporated is approaching the 21st Century with the goal of becoming a total media-communications company, using music, software, video, printed music, books, and electronic media to enhance the believer's personal relationship with God.

You may contact Integrity at:

Integrity Incorporated
1000 Cody Road
Mobile, Alabama 36695-3425

334-633-9000 (phone)
334-633-5202 (fax)

Visit Integrity's website:
www.integritymusic.com

or

Contact Integrity by e-mail:
cservice@integinc.com

Additional copies of this book and other titles
from ALBURY PUBLISHING are
available at your local bookstore.

ALBURY PUBLISHING

P. O. Box 470406

Tulsa, Oklahoma 74147-0406

For International and Canadian orders,
please contact

Access Sales International
2448 East 81st Street
Suite 4900
Tulsa, OK 74137
Phone 918-523-5590   Fax 918-496-2822

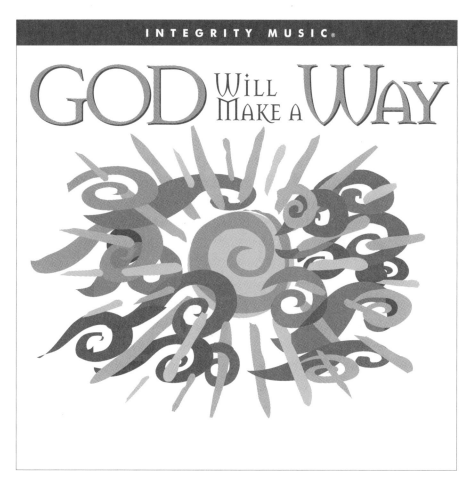

*Available in CD and cassette at your
local Christian bookstore.*